D1261424

Knowledge Management
Processes and Technologies

KNOWLEDGE MANAGEMENT
Processes and Technologies

HERWIG ROLLETT

Kluwer Academic Publishers
Boston/Dordrecht/London

658.4038
R75k

Distributors for North, Central and South America:
Kluwer Academic Publishers
101 Philip Drive
Assinippi Park
Norwell, Massachusetts 02061 USA
Telephone (781) 871-6600
Fax (781) 681-9045
E-Mail: kluwer@wkap.com

Distributors for all other countries:
Kluwer Academic Publishers Group
Post Office Box 322
3300 AH Dordrecht, THE NETHERLANDS
Telephone 31 786 576 000
Fax 31 786 576 254
E-Mail: services@wkap.nl

 Electronic Services <http://www.wkap.nl>

Library of Congress Cataloging-in-Publication Data

KNOWLEDGE MANAGEMENT:
PROCESSES AND TECHNOLOGIES
Herwig Rollett
ISBN 1-4020-7169-8

A C.I.P. Catalogue record for this book is available
from the Library of Congress.

Copyright © 2003 by Kluwer Academic Publishers

All rights reserved. No part of this work may be reproduced, stored in a retrieval
system, or transmitted in any form or by any means, electronic, mechanical,
photocopying, microfilming, recording, or otherwise, without written permission
from the Publisher, with the exception of any material supplied specifically for the
purpose of being entered and executed on a computer system, for exclusive use by
the purchaser of the work.

Permission for books published in Europe: permissions@wkap.nl
Permissions for books published in the United States of America: permissions@wkap.com

Printed on acid-free paper.

Printed in the United States of America

Contents

University Libraries
Carnegie Mellon University
Pittsburgh, PA 15213-3890

Foreword

The transitions to a knowledge society and a global knowledge economy will be the most important social and economic changes in the twenty-first century. The global knowledge economy with its high innovation speed and an increasing demand of innovative and knowledge intensive products and services calls for new management tools and methods. Since the primary key to growth in our economy is innovation, which in turn is enabled through knowledge, efficient knowledge management tools and methods have become imperative for almost all types of organizations.

Talking about knowledge management raises the question of what "knowledge" is. Since Aristotle's essential distinction between "know-what" and "know-how" humankind has been thinking about a definition for the term "knowledge". But a definition on which everybody agrees does not exist yet and will probably never exist. Still, the following sample of definitions for knowledge try to offer you some guidance:

- *Knowledge is identified, classified, and valid information.*

- *Knowledge is information in contextualized action.*

- *Knowledge is the mapping from reality, states, and activities onto the internal model of the "real" world, which an individual or an organization has. With this internal model an individual or an organization can make statements about reality.*

- *Explicit knowledge is knowledge that can be formalized and codified. Tacit knowledge is difficult to articulate in writing and is acquired through personal experience.*

With this in mind, knowledge management can be defined as follows. *Knowledge management deals with*

- *knowledge-friendly environments in which knowledge can develop and flourish to provide individuals, organizations, or regions with*

- *context-sensitive knowledge and*

- *the ability of knowledge workers to apply the knowledge for action.*

Knowledge management can be addressed from two different perspectives. The first perspective is more people-oriented as it focuses on people and organizations. The second perspective places the emphasis on information technologies as enabling technologies. The difference between these two perspectives is the level at which knowledge management is applied:

In people-oriented knowledge management, the focus is on the people, the organization and the associated working and communication processes rather than on the technology. People-oriented knowledge management seeks answers to questions such as "How can we improve the knowledge creation and organization?", "How can we adapt our communication culture to become more knowledge-friendly?", "How can we manage our human capital more efficiently?", and "What methods and incentives exist to foster knowledge sharing and transfer?"

The objective of technology-oriented knowledge management is to support knowledge workers in companies at an operational level. That is, information technologies are used as enabling technology to provide the knowledge somebody needs to perform a specific task as efficiently as possible. Often, this requires a careful and smooth integration of knowledge management tools with business process management tools.

This book reflects these different perspectives with two parts dealing with knowledge management processes (part II) and the role of information technologies to support these processes (part III).

Thanks to the sound experience the author, Herwig Rollett, has gained in many knowledge management research and industry projects, you are offered much support and advice if you plan to introduce knowledge management in your organization. Of particular value is that the book does not only suggest "what" methods can be introduced, but also "how" they can be introduced—which brings us back to Aristotle who argued that knowledge comprises both the "know-what" and the "know-how". In this sense, this book is a huge treasure of knowledge about knowledge management.

So as you read this book, I suggest you keep the overall intention of knowledge management in mind: The provision of knowledge-friendly cultures and working environments. If you follow this advice, this book will help continually shaping your thinking in the way required for the success of your organization in the new knowledge economy.

Klaus Tochtermann
CEO, Know-Center Graz

Preface

The first thing I discovered when I started out in knowledge management was that it is *not* about technology. It is about people. People as individuals, people as teams, people as communities, people as organizations.

The second thing I discovered was that technology, handled properly, *can* make an important contribution. It can connect people with each other. It can connect people to information they find useful. It can protect them from irrelevant content. Sometimes, systems can even come up with something one is tempted to call knowledge on their own.

The third thing I discovered was that there was no book providing a compact, comprehensive, balanced overview of both knowledge management and the role technology could—or should—play. A book that would discuss knowledge management processes, point out the most important issues, and assess the relevance of technologies to the various processes. Without going to unnecessary lengths. And in an easily accessible way.

I occupied myself with knowledge management in its various forms: With a strategic focus and with an operational focus, with a people focus and with a technology focus, with an organizational focus and with a personal focus. Meanwhile, the hype around knowledge management grew, as did the jungle of theories, models, methods, practices, and tools of knowledge management. Books on the subject were springing up like mushrooms. Except, of course, the kind of book I considered the most appropriate as a guide through that jungle.

At some point, I found myself writing the book I had been missing when I first started out. You are holding the result in your hands. If you are taking your first steps in knowledge management, it will provide you with a valuable map of the territory. And even if you are already an expert, I am confident that you will discover a few aspects which you have not yet considered in this light.

Books are written by authors. But authors would rarely write books if it were not for the encouragement and support of many people. I am particularly grateful to all my colleagues at the Know-Center and at the Institute for Information Processing and Computer-Supported New Media at Graz University of Technology, not only for supporting me in writing this book, but also for providing a very pleasant working environment. Special thanks go to Hermann Maurer, Klaus Tochtermann, Tobias Ley, Markus Strohmaier, Janez Hrastnik, Andreas Ausserhofer, and Denis Helic. The Know-Center is a Competence Center funded within the Austrian K plus Competence Centers Program (www.kplus.at) under the auspices of the Austrian Ministry of Transport, Innovation and Technology.

Many further people have directly or indirectly helped to make this book possible: The members of Wissensmanagement Forum and its PhD circle; people from the companies I have conducted projects with; the members of the Forschung Austria taskforce on knowledge management; all the people with whom I discussed knowledge management issues at conferences, workshops, and informal meetings; and last but not least my friends and family. I would particularly like to thank, in alphabetical order, Manfred Bornemann, Georg Droschl, Marion Graggober, Karin Grasenick, Erich Hartlieb, Herbert Haubold, Bernd Humpl, Thomas Jud, Iris Klein, Ulrike Krießmann, Philipp Koronakis, Karl-Heinz Leitner, Thomas Mikl, Fritz Ohler, Johann Ortner, Franz Pirker, Maja Pivec, Michael Ploder, Arthur Primus, Karl Ritsch, Günter Rollett, Martin Sammer, Andreas Schibany, Gerald Steiner, Josef Tuppinger, Patrick Wehinger, Reinhard Willfort, and Kurt Wöls. Finally, I would like to thank my publishers, particularly Lance Wobus.

Ultimately, a book like this has to be judged by its usefulness to the reader. Most of all, therefore, I hope that it will help you.

HERWIG ROLLETT

I

BACKGROUND

Chapter 1

Introduction

The herd is grazing near a small river. A light wind is blowing over the plain. The hunters are lying low behind a ridge, in small groups. They are good hunters: They know where to hide so the herd cannot smell them. Together, they move. The tribe will have a feast tonight.

The elders of the tribe are pleased. Another successful hunt. They encourage the hunters to recount the story to the children.

Under the guidance of the elders, the tribe has flourished. When resolving disputes, they try to be fair. But ultimately, their responsibility is to the future of the tribe. Occasionally, the elders favor those hunters who are not just quick and strong, but also unusually smart. And the people who have proved adept at finding fruit in abundance. And the old one who knows how to heal, and his apprentice. In a sense, they are managing knowledge.

In the boardroom of a multinational manufacturing company, the directors are pleased. Since the company is competing on price, its knowledge management initiative has focused on increasing efficiency by sharing lessons learned between plants all over the world. Costs have been reduced by improving cycle times and avoiding common mistakes.

First, the responsible managers in the plants have been encouraged to regularly visit other plants. This has helped them establish a shared perspective with their peers as well as a level of trust. Only then has technology been introduced to support the process: Lessons learned are collected on a central server and classified for easy retrieval. All of them contain relevant contact details for further inquiries. In addition, an existing suggestion scheme has been brought up to date and linked to incentives.

The criminal investigation department

The head of a criminal investigation department is pleased. The magic word is knowledge discovery: Leads extracted from the aggregated content of various databases with the help of the new data mining system have already led to five arrests.

Training his officers works well, too. The rules and procedures of police work, and some of the required background knowledge, are written down and taught in courses. Beyond this explicit knowledge lies the tacit knowledge officers have accumulated through personal experience. People find it hard to articulate, and often are not even aware of what they know. These things cannot be taught, but police officers pick them up over time from their partners.

The software company

The chief executive of a medium sized software company is pleased. He co-founded the business four years ago and has presided over its rapid growth to almost two hundred staff. The downside of growth showed when it became apparent that unlike the close-knit group they were in the early days, employees suddenly did not even know what others were doing any more.

Looking at the situation through the lens of knowledge management, however, quickly revealed a number of simple measures the company could take. There is now a large common room, where programmers gather around the coffee machine. Regular trips into the countryside allow employees to catch up with each other in an informal atmosphere. A job rotation scheme has been met with approval by most employees. More attention is now also being paid to recruiting to avoid unnecessary fragmentation.

The company, even though it is itself developing software, has resisted the temptation of turning to information technology as a solution too early. Yellow pages providing details on the skills and experience of employees, and even automated expertise profiling, have been discussed. However, they will not be implemented until the benefits really outweigh the effort.

The call center

The manager of a call center providing customer support is pleased. On the one hand, sharing and reusing knowledge systematically with a helpdesk application has increased customer satisfaction by reducing the time employees need to answer inquiries, and by increasing the quality of the answers. Since employee turnover is high at the call center, the most important experiences have been packaged into an eLearning course, which keeps costs for training new hires down.

On the other hand, the manager has also succeeded in his second mission: To improve the collection and use of knowledge about customers. The new customer relationship management software generates customer profiles. Employees answering calls receive relevant background information about customers in a user-friendly interface, integrated with that of the helpdesk application.

The owner-manager of a small engineering company is pleased. As specialists in a niche market, he and his team are successfully staying ahead of the competition through research and innovation. To them, knowledge management has always been an integral part of what they do.

The small engineering company

Their focus is not so much on efficiency, but rather on the effectiveness of creating and integrating knowledge. They employ creativity techniques, attend many conferences, and cooperate closely with both industry and scientific partners. Technologies like intelligent agents, automatic text summarization, and visualization help them find, filter, and make sense of the vast amount of documented knowledge available.

Knowledge Management: What and Why

The increasing complexity of both the environment in which companies operate and of their internal workings, combined with the speed demanded from them, the pressure for innovation, and the scarcity of attention as the ultimate limited resource, make knowledge central to business success today. Knowledge is now seen as a factor of production not only on par with land, labor, and capital, but surpassing them in importance.

Importance of knowledge

How should we think about knowledge? It is frequently pictured at the top of a hierarchy, with information below it and data at the bottom. Various criteria have been suggested to distinguish knowledge from information and data, including value (knowledge is more valuable than information and

Data, information, knowledge

data), temporal sequence (knowledge is based on information, which in turn is based on data), the role of structure, context, and interpretation (knowledge is structured, contextualized, and interpreted information), and the potential for action (knowledge, unlike information, can be directly acted upon).

Without doubt, these criteria may sharpen one's awareness of important aspects. However, clear-cut definitions of knowledge tend to be either too restrictive, obscuring one's view, or too broad to offer much guidance in practice. It is therefore advisable not to let a single definition guide one's exploration of knowledge management.

Where is knowledge located? First of all, knowledge is held by people: By individuals, teams, communities, and organizational units. Relationships between people and between items of content also contain knowledge, as do physical arrangements such as floor layouts. Some knowledge has been documented in patents, books, journals, magazines, reports, presentations, manuals, memos, meeting minutes, problem-solution lists, newsfeeds, and databases. Business processes, best practices, lessons learned, common mistakes, design rationales, stories, and learning histories represent knowledge which may or may not have been documented. Finally, knowledge is also embedded in software and equipment.

Emergence of knowledge management

Ever more knowledge is available, and access to much of that knowledge is getting ever better thanks to technology. Knowledge management has emerged as a label for consciously perceiving and addressing the issues raised by the importance and the availability of knowledge. It consists of more than directly managing knowledge as a resource: It is concerned with managing the environment of knowledge workers, with creating and maintaining favorable conditions for value creation based on knowledge.

Many sources

Knowledge management is not a discipline with well defined boundaries. The examples above, from the tribe to the engineering company, illustrate the scope of the subject. It draws on many different fields of study, including business studies, psychology, sociology, educational science, cognitive science, computer science, and library and information science. It concerns strategic management, organizational development, business process management, human resources management, communications management, information technology management, change management, and controlling. Practitioners in companies, consultants, system vendors, and academics each address the subject in their own way.

Definitions of knowledge management are legion, and many of them contradict each other. This book does not attempt to squeeze knowledge management into a neatly defined box. Instead, it provides an overview of what knowledge management is all about by discussing relevant issues. Knowledge management is best seen as a way of thinking. After reading this book, you will have that way of thinking at your disposal.

A way of thinking

Part I continues with chapter 2, which introduces two different but complementary ways to think about knowledge management: In terms of processes, and in terms of interactions. Chapter 3 then summarizes lessons learned from past knowledge management projects, which are used to motivate discussions throughout the book.

The structure of this book

Part II contains one chapter for each of the knowledge management processes. Part III discusses the role of technologies in knowledge management, each chapter providing an overview of the technology in question, a discussion of its relevance to knowledge management, and an examination of open issues and opportunities for future research and development. Part III closes with a summary of the contribution of technologies to knowledge management.

Chapter 2

Two Complementary Views

The most common type of knowledge management framework is based on identifying a number of different processes and then taking those as the foundation for further discussions. Many frameworks of this kind have been proposed as experience has shown their usefulness [97, 146]. Superficially, most of these process-based frameworks appear fairly similar. The differences lie in the details and can be attributed to the intended use of the framework in question.

This chapter introduces a process view of knowledge management created for the purpose of structuring this book. Each process and its associated issues are discussed in greater detail in part II of this book, where there is one chapter for each process. In part III, the process view is employed to judge the relevance of various technologies: Each chapter assesses the extent to which the technologies in question contribute to each of the processes introduced here.

There are, however, some aspects that are not easily conveyed by any purely process-based view. After explaining the process view, this chapter therefore introduces the interaction view. That view, too, is used in various guises throughout the rest of this book, including symbols in the margins indicating what kind of interaction the corresponding paragraphs are about.

The Process View

Using knowledge plays a central role in two ways. First, the goal of all knowledge management processes ultimately is to

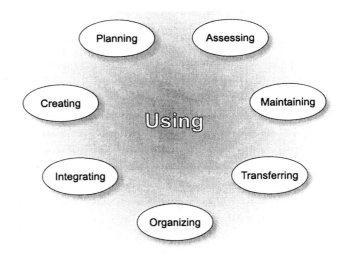

Figure 2.1.   The process view of knowledge management.

Using
knowledge is
means and end

optimize the way knowledge is used. And second, knowledge is of course being used in each all of those processes. Using knowledge cannot be meaningfully separated from other processes. It is simultaneously the means and the end of knowledge management.

The process view acknowledges this by symbolically placing the use of knowledge at its center, but refraining from treating it as a separate process (Figure 2.1). Floating around it are the processes of knowledge planning, creating knowledge, integrating knowledge, organizing knowledge, transferring knowledge, maintaining knowledge, and assessing knowledge. The arrangement of those processes is not meant to indicate any linear sequence. While some processes may typically follow others, there are in fact many more connections between those processes than could reasonably be visualized.

Knowledge management does not exist in a vacuum. It is always tied to the particular situation of an organization and a business environment. Therefore, knowledge planning is of paramount importance for any knowledge management initiative.

Specific goals have to be established for each knowledge management effort, and these goals must link those efforts to the overall business strategy. General performance targets can be complemented by knowledge targets. A knowledge management strategy sets the direction for reaching those knowledge goals. Apart from all that, knowledge planning also helps to uncover the expectations of all the parties involved and to build consensus and commitment.

Knowledge planning is, however, more than a one-off event limited to the first phase of a knowledge management initiative. It should be an ongoing activity and firmly embedded in organizational practices as a matter of course, consisting not just of checking established goals, but also of periodically revisiting those goals and adapting them as well as the knowledge management strategy where necessary.

There are basically two ways for an organization to increase its overall stock of knowledge: By creating new knowledge, and by acquiring already existing knowledge. Knowledge creation may happen deliberately, for instance in research labs dedicated to new product development, or it may happen more or less accidentally, for instance when employees stumble upon innovative ways to perform their work.

Managing the former is already quite a challenge, but the latter cannot be managed directly at all. Therefore, managing knowledge creation first and foremost means establishing conditions under which knowledge is likely to be created, for instance by providing a stimulating environment, making sure people are aware of methods and tools aiding creativity, and generally fostering an organizational culture which emphasizes open minds.

This is, of course, not just a question of encouraging experimentation. It also means that employees must have both the time necessary for trying new approaches and be secure in the knowledge that the setbacks that will invariably occur along with the successes will be seen as valuable learning experiences rather than as mistakes.

Integrating knowledge comprises all the ways in which already existing knowledge can be made available to the organization. On the one hand, this includes acquiring knowledge from external sources, for instance by recruiting new staff, having employees attend conferences, hiring consultants, establishing joint ventures, buying knowledge products like market research reports or software, or simply gathering knowledge from open sources.

On the other hand, it also includes integrating knowledge that already exists within the company, for example by capturing knowledge that might otherwise be lost, and discovering knowledge that has not been previously recognized as such in corporate repositories. If the knowledge to be integrated resides in the heads of employees, their willingness to share that knowledge becomes an important issue.

Organizing knowledge adds value by establishing different kinds of structures for the knowledge available to an organization. Typically, this would mean determining the context of given items of knowledge and then structuring them for instance through hierarchical classification or knowledge mapping.

Knowledge transfer refers to the deliberate and planned exchange of knowledge as well as to ad hoc sharing of knowledge. A typical example for knowledge transfer would be internal training.

Determining the most appropriate way to transfer knowledge depends both on the source and on the intended receiver. If the knowledge to be transferred resides in a computer system, important aspects include retrieval mechanisms, push approaches and the form of presentation. Transferring tacit knowledge presents a particular challenge.

Knowledge maintenance consists of reviewing, correcting and updating, refining, preserving, and removing knowledge. This concerns both the knowledge in peoples' heads and the content and structure of repositories. The question of who should be responsible for knowledge maintenance frequently turns out to be far from easy to answer.

Knowledge assessment can take several forms. At the level of individual knowledge items, quality ratings can be assigned for criteria like relevance, accuracy, comprehensiveness, and timeliness. At a higher level of abstraction, intellectual capital is measured to convey an overall picture of the knowledge available to a company. Finally, tying this process back to knowledge planning, knowledge assessment also means checking the extent to which knowledge targets have been reached.

As an example for all those processes, consider the case of a company that has decided to place more emphasis on new product development. It now has to consider how to ensure the availability and appropriate use of the necessary knowledge (knowledge planning). A workshop results in the formulation of a concept for a new product (creating knowledge). Not only that concept, but also the design rationale behind it and the lessons learned from the process are documented and stored in a repository (integrating knowledge). They are also assigned appropriate classification codes, making their retrieval easier in the future, and a pointer to them is placed on the corporate knowledge map (organizing knowledge).

Example:
New product
development

The participants of another workshop in a different department are now aware of the work that has been done and they can easily access that knowledge, either by retrieving the documents from the repository or by looking up who was involved and talking to those people (transferring knowledge). As soon as the results of the next workshop are in, they are compared with the previous ones and some of the latter receive links to related, more up-to-date content (maintaining knowledge). Finally, the knowledge generated and managed this way is reflected in the company's intellectual capital report (assessing knowledge).

This example can also be used to demonstrate that the knowledge management processes are often also connected in ways that defy any attempt to establish a linear sequence. Identifying suitable participants for the workshop (knowledge planning), for instance, may rely on previously created expertise profiles (creating knowledge and assessing knowledge). Similarly, the classification of the lessons learned (organizing knowledge) relies on an up-to-date classification scheme (maintaining knowledge).

The Interaction View

Knowledge management is very much about communication, and analyzing and discussing this topic only from the perspective of the processes outlined in the previous section does not do justice to the significance of the various forms of communication involved. In particular, it is important to consider how the different agents interact with each other. Purely process-based views do not specifically encourage this since

Importance of
communication

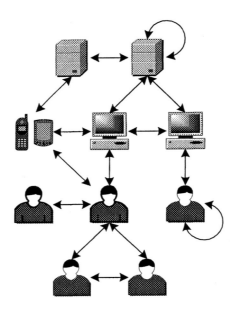

Figure 2.2.   The interaction view of knowledge management.

the different agents and their relationships are not obvious. For this reason, the process view is complemented by the interaction view (Figure 2.2).

Interactions
highlight issues

This view shows a number of persons and computer systems as well as arrows symbolizing interactions between them. There are five people, two personal computers, a mobile device, and two servers, all interacting with each other in various ways. Of course, a framework like this cannot encompass all the possibilities for interactions without becoming too complex to be of much use in practice. On the other hand, the inclusion of several different entities in this view immediately suggests a number of issues which would not be obvious if some of its components were lumped together.

First, some of the people talk to each other and some do not. There is a group of people in which everybody talks to everybody else. This may be, for example, a project team, employees sharing a room, or a community of practice. There is also another person connected to that group through only one of its members. This raises the question of gatekeeper functions. Finally, there is a person who never talks to the others face-to-face at all. Their communication must be supported by appropriate technology.

These are important considerations for any knowledge management effort: Identifying formal and, even more importantly, informal networks of people, identifying barriers to communication, and planning the knowledge management initiative accordingly. This becomes even more crucial for the design of supporting information technology, since computers are generally less flexible than people in working around a lack of shared context.

The person with the curved arrow symbolizes thinking as a kind of interaction with oneself. This will be of particular importance in the context of knowledge creation.

Looking at interactions between people and systems, one can see a person interacting not only with a personal computer, but also with mobile devices, for instance a personal digital assistant and a mobile phone.

This raises a number of issues concerning the interaction between people and information technology for knowledge management, such as the appropriateness of user interfaces, the importance of the display size for visualization techniques, and the trade-off between the costs of supporting technically very different platforms on the one hand and the benefits of enabling mobile knowledge management support on the other.

Interactions between computers also take a number of forms. Of course personal computers interact with servers in a variety of ways. Additionally, the arrow between two personal computers indicates peer-to-peer computing, which is based on direct communication between personal computers and is increasingly being used for knowledge management. The question arises which type of interaction is better suited for which knowledge management purposes.

The interaction view also indicates the need for synchronization between personal computers and mobile devices as well as interactions between mobile devices and servers, for instance in the case of using online services through wireless data connections.

Servers interact with each other as well as with personal computers. This raises issues like deciding which knowledge management tasks are best performed by which system, for instance in the case of content aggregation. Finally, the curved arrow attached to a server indicates that value can also be added to content through advanced information processing techniques.

Knowledge flows

By showing different interactions of people with each other, of people and systems, and of systems with each other, the interaction view prompts one to think about the different ways in which knowledge can be communicated in these constellations.

Between people, knowledge may be transferred explicitly, for instance by a teacher in a classroom. Alternatively, implicit knowledge transfer means that the person who is learning something new does so by observing someone else at work, perhaps without even being aware of it. For the transfer of tacit knowledge, this is often the only realistic method. A typical example for the importance of this kind of knowledge transfer would be apprenticeships in the crafts.

In between purely explicit and purely implicit knowledge transfer lies the everyday event of someone observing something and then asking a question. Appropriately designed work processes can make knowledge transfer a natural by-product of work and are therefore invaluable for all types of knowledge transfer involving an implicit component.

Flows of knowledge between people and systems can also be understood in terms of explicit and implicit knowledge transfer. Apart from the obvious possibility of someone explicitly and deliberately adding knowledge to the system, the system could also observe the user's behavior and implicitly collect valuable knowledge that way. The challenge here of course lies in analyzing the data about the user's behavior to the extent where it makes sense to speak of the results as knowledge.

Again, appropriately designed work processes can provide some middle ground by making it relatively easy for the system to capture knowledge while simultaneously reducing the effort necessary on the part of the user, for whom this is merely a by-product of work he is carrying out anyway, rather than a separate task.

The transfer of knowledge from a system to a user may be initiated by either of them. If it is the user who initiates the interaction, this is called knowledge pull. If it is the system, this is a case of knowledge push. In the context of knowledge management, this includes not only classical push methods through media like email, but also the possibility for the system to interrupt the user's work in order to alert him to a piece of knowledge relevant to his current task. The most interesting aspect here lies in how the system can decide whether or not it makes sense to interrupt the user.

The term interaction emphasizes both directions of communication. Consider the case of an employee writing a proposal for a project and interrupting her work to retrieve some files from the company's intranet containing background information about another company. At first sight, this may look like a typical example of explicit knowledge transfer from the system to the employee.

However, the reverse direction may be even more interesting: The system may be observing the user's actions and may be able to infer a link between the project and that other company, which could be a valuable bit of knowledge, while the content of the files the user retrieved might not even justify the term knowledge.

Turning to knowledge flows between systems, the interaction view suggests that one should consider issues arising out of the different kinds of such flows, ranging from straightforward replication to more demanding issues such as how to best distribute tasks like postprocessing and visualization of search results between the server and the client.

Finally, particularly interesting interactions between systems are those which allow a system to actually create new knowledge. This may happen either through analyzing unstructured information and extracting knowledge, or through processing already formalized knowledge.

Each of these three types of interactions—people to people, people to systems, and systems to systems—is important to almost all of the knowledge management processes. Knowledge planning, as a strategic activity, is special in that it usually does not directly involve information technology support.

Processes rely on interactions

Knowledge creation is primarily based on interactions between people as well, but also stands to gain from supporting systems. Integrating knowledge naturally has to cover all types of interactions in order to accomplish its purpose of making knowledge available to the entire company. Organizing knowledge necessarily involves information technology today—the days of large libraries being managed by shuffling bits of paper are gone. Knowledge transfer, again, by its very nature has to support all types of interactions. Knowledge maintenance and knowledge assessment also depend on each type of interaction.

The fact that almost all processes rely on all types of interactions and that one cannot easily subsume either of them under the other also demonstrates that it does indeed make sense to regard processes and interactions as separate dimensions, as distinct and useful ways to look at issues in knowledge management.

Chapter 3

Lessons Learned from Past Projects

Knowledge management as a topic has attracted a lot of interest in the past few years, and many knowledge management projects have already been conducted in various organizations. Some were outstanding successes, others dismal failures. From the wealth of experiences gained in those projects, valuable lessons can be learned. With the help of these lessons learned, approaching knowledge management is less guesswork based on purely theoretical models, and more grounded in practical experience.

For that reason, this chapter summarizes important lessons learned from past knowledge management projects. While such a collection can never be exhaustive, it provides a valuable overview of the most important issues to be addressed and pitfalls to be avoided.

This is not the first book published on the subject of knowledge management; it is a second generation book in the sense that it builds on these lessons learned. The lessons are used to motivate both theoretical considerations and practical advice. Throughout the book, these lessons learned are referred to in order to point out the proven practical relevance of various aspects of the discussions.

Fundamental Lessons Learned

The first and most general lesson learned is that knowledge management is always primarily about people. In everything you propose to do as part of a knowledge management effort, think about the people first: The ones who have knowledge,

KM is primarily about people

the ones who need knowledge, the ones who will benefit from what you propose, the ones who might perceive their situation as worsening, the ones who will have to implement changes, and the ones who will have to support them.

People are important because it is in their heads that most knowledge resides [53]. Many important facets of knowledge management efforts are purely people-based, for instance internal communication programs [143]. Successful knowledge sharing communities depend on people networks much more than on information technology networks [82]. Consider the people systems surrounding the technology systems [123]. People have to be seen both as providers and as consumers of content. The biggest costs of knowledge management projects are usually associated with the people who add value to that content, make it accessible, and help others find it [10].

KM should be holistic and comprehensive

A narrow focus on a particular aspect of knowledge management will not lead to success. Knowledge management has to be addressed in its entirety [131]. It has to be approached in a holistic fashion [82]. A holistic approach will be integrated across the organization [124] and pay attention to the interrelationship between processes like knowledge sharing, knowledge creation, and organizational change [156].

Balances have to be struck

While it is clear that knowledge management should be a comprehensive undertaking and that people should always come first, the precise balance between a culture focus, a leadership focus, an organizational structure focus, a process focus, a content focus, a learning focus, and a technology focus has to be determined for each particular organization [56, 82, 87].

This is intimately connected with another balance to be struck: The balance between providing better access to existing knowledge and a paradigm emphasizing organizational learning and knowledge creation [124, 156].

Attempts to enable the efficient reuse of knowledge, usually with the help of information technology, have to be balanced against the need for individualized offerings, which sometimes can only be provided by other people [46].

Lessons Learned about Planning

First, determine whether the problems to be addressed are in fact of a knowledge-based nature and can therefore really be solved by knowledge management [56]. The planning phase itself should begin with an open-minded examination of the current situation, and not with a solution-based model [131]. Knowledge management planning should support assumption surfacing [161] and strive to create win-win situations between company interests and the concerns of individual knowledge workers [79].

Planning is important

One popular expectation to avoid is that once organizational changes or new systems are in place, people will happily flock to the new ways of working: "Build it and they'll come". In fact, they won't [151]. In addressing this issue, planning should not only rely on incentive schemes, but also shift the focus from collecting to reusing knowledge [47].

Since the promises of knowledge management often create a lot of excitement and anticipation, it is particularly important not to get carried away, but to plan what can realistically be implemented with available resources [123].

Careful planning is also a precaution against problems related to the lack commitment from all involved parties, which tend to be numerous in knowledge management projects [22]. In the past, projects with significant investments in planning had higher impact than those without [75].

Understand your knowledge requirements from a strategic perspective [179]. This will enable you to identify which knowledge is critical and where that knowledge originates [131]. Taking stock of existing knowledge, you will also recognize the most significant knowledge gaps [161]. A comprehensive analysis phase is instrumental in ensuring the project will stay on target, in budget, and balanced [56].

Understand the knowledge requirements

Organizations often suffer from a lack of shared understanding of the meaning of knowledge management [59]. It may be impossible to come up with a definition that everybody will be completely happy with, but that must not be an excuse for not clarifying what is meant by the term. Try to develop a working definition of knowledge management [53]. This working definition need not live up to academic standards, but it has to be based on the consensus of all involved parties. Beware of definitions that are extremely broad and politically correct, and therefore in all likelihood practically useless [161]. A brief definition alone may not be enough to create a shared understanding of the concept. Architectures,

Ensure agreement on what is meant by KM

models, and strategies can also help to establish common ground [10].

**Have a clear
KM strategy**

As with all organizational change projects, clear goals and a clear strategy are essential for knowledge management projects [8, 10, 87]. A potential stumbling block in this context are personal intentions of employees that are incoherent with company interests [46]. Successful projects often deliberately exclude certain issues from their charters [39].

**KM strategy and
business
strategy must
be linked**

Knowledge management must not be perceived as an end in itself [131]. While there should be a distinct knowledge management strategy, it must of course be aligned with and firmly linked to the overall business strategy of the organization [87, 179].

**Communicate
the KM strategy**

A knowledge management strategy not only serves planning purposes. It also needs to be communicated to all those who in the end are expected to behave differently [123, 156]. Objectives are most effectively communicated by management [131]. The way language is used plays an important role here [39].

**Link KM to
business results**

Be clear about exactly what you are trying to achieve. This may be revenue generation, but also the improvement of internal efficiency. Think about the potential benefits from the perspective of the concerned knowledge consumers [124]. Money saved or earned is of course the most impressive benefit for management, but business results can also be demonstrated through more indirect measures such as reduced cycle times and or increased customer satisfaction [39]. The responsibility for establishing the link between knowledge management and concrete business results should lie with senior management [8].

Start small

Plan on getting your knowledge management project off the ground by starting small [124]. Rather than worrying about imperfections, treat any approach as provisional [10]. Risks should be limited through a cautious phase-in approach with well-defined deliverables [56, 59]. Prototyping often helps to clarify requirements, to test capabilities, and to gain buy-in [87].

**Conduct a
pilot project**

Conduct a pilot project [118]. This not only requires smaller investments, but also makes it possible to initially focus one's efforts on a suitable pilot group with measurable objectives. Assign quality staff to the pilot full-time, since part-time initiatives may be perceived as not important to management [34]. Plan the pilot in a way that will show measurable results in less than six months [131].

Do not make the mistake of starting with a low-profile project to "test the waters" [5]. Instead, address critical business issues that have a high pay-off right from the start [123].

Address critical business issues from the start

Lessons Learned about Leadership

In order to obtain buy-in, the short-term impact of a project needs to be demonstrated both to managers and to end-users [161]. Make added capability and cost-containment obvious to senior management and enhance the project's visibility by associating it with events like seminars and visits of experts [22]. Quantify the impact of the project by specifying how performance will change. Build a business case that is both relevant and believable [56].

Evangelize and obtain buy-in

Buy-in from the user community is best obtained through an articulate and technically literate advocate rooted in that community [22]. Communicate how knowledge management will meet the daily needs of users [10]. Evangelizing may be the task of a specially created role of knowledge champion or become a task of all leaders [35]. The most convincing arguments once the project is off the ground are of course early successes. Benchmarking may not be cheap, but it may help to create a sense of urgency and to demonstrate the value of external sources of knowledge [123].

Knowledge leaders have to consistently and constantly reinforce the central messages of knowledge management [123]. They must be proactive themselves rather than assuming that someone else will take the initiative [5]. Knowledge leaders need the charisma to recruit believers, both upstream and downstream [59]. They also have to be seen to practice what they preach [151].

Have appropriate KM leaders

The costs of implementing knowledge management can be a significant barrier [41]. It is up to management to provide the necessary funding and other resources to knowledge management initiatives in time [39, 46].

Management has to provide funding

Management's role should not be limited to sponsorship, but include active participation as well [131]. In particular, management should help define the goals of the project [34], identify which kinds of knowledge are the most important ones to the company [39] and generally focus the knowledge management effort on the core business priorities [8].

Management should actively participate

Management should not only endorse the knowledge management effort, but actually push it forward [143]. Active participation is also required for rewarding behavior that is to be reinforced, for instance by promoting the right people [123].

Management should communicate commitment

The priorities and objectives of a knowledge management initiative are most effectively communicated by management [123, 131]. This includes clearly identifying knowledge management as a mainstream corporate development effort [34] and showing employees that management is thoroughly convinced of its importance for the company's success [39, 46].

Management must walk the talk

As always, talk alone is not enough. It is often important that management acts as an example rather than just as a facilitator of knowledge management [79]. Walking the talk also means that management must give up knowledge hoarding first [46]. Furthermore, leading by example enables management to get valuable feedback [123].

Management can help remove barriers

One of the most important tasks for management is to remove barriers to progress, particularly when it comes to attitudes such as the not-invented-here syndrome. Success stories are a good way to break the mold [123]. Management must also give employees the time they need for communication, reflection, and networking [46]. Significant changes to business processes may be necessary [151].

Top management really needs to be involved

Senior management support is essential for any knowledge management effort [34, 41, 156]. Company-wide, transformation-oriented projects, in particular, require support from top management, as does the process of tying a knowledge management initiative to top management's vision [123, 39].

Lessons Learned about Culture

Organizational culture is absolutely crucial

Organizational culture is of crucial importance for all knowledge management projects [8, 35, 46]. Knowledge management will not get anywhere unless the knowledge workers concerned are willing to take part in it [79]. Organizational culture is a key driver and inhibitor of knowledge sharing [123]. An appropriate culture is a question of balance. Openness is needed, but must not degenerate into chaos. Fighting entrenched corporate cultures and creating a knowledge-friendly culture is not only one of the most important factors for success, but probably also the most difficult of all challenges in introducing knowledge management, particularly since it cannot be compensated for by technology, content, or project management [39, 59].

Organizational culture should stress the value of knowledge for both the individual employee and the company as a whole. Everybody should be aware of the fact that most of that value resides in the minds of the employees [59]. A positive orientation to knowledge is indicated by employees who display not only intelligence, but also curiosity and a willingness to explore and learn both on and off the job, who look to experience and expertise and not only hierarchy, and by executives who encourage the creation and use of knowledge [39].

Foster a positive orientation to knowledge

Valuing personal expertise is important, but it must not stand in the way of sharing [124]. Organizational culture should therefore promote knowledge sharing [124, 56]. Most importantly, this includes dispelling employees' fears that sharing their knowledge will erode their power or, in the long run, even cost them their jobs [39, 46]. Through an appropriate culture, knowledge sharing and usage may lead to greater power, both formal and informal, than hoarding knowledge [35].

Dispel fears of sharing

The potential value of knowledge can only be realized if it is really being used. The actual use of available knowledge needs to be promoted. This is especially true for the use of knowledge from outside sources: The not-invented-here syndrome has to be overcome [46]. Benchmarking often helps to change this kind of culture [123].

Promote knowledge use

Collaboration will happen all by itself to some extent, but the level required for effective knowledge management will not be attained without an appropriate culture [56]. In order to be able to collaborate, share knowledge, and learn from each other effectively, employees first and foremost must relate to each other as people [82].

Promote collaboration

The transfer of new and innovative knowledge will be severely curtailed if the dominant culture is one of conflict avoidance [46]. Conflict should be valued not only in order to capitalize on such knowledge, but also because properly resolved conflicts themselves frequently generate new knowledge and innovation [35].

Value conflict

The importance of experimentation must not be underes-

Accept mistakes

timated [53]. This implies the need for a culture in which mistakes are accepted rather than penalized [46].

Promote trust

Successful knowledge management will require a high level of trust among employees. Knowledge sharing, in particular, is enabled by trust reducing fears that others will act opportunistically [46].

Influence culture through recruiting and training

Use recruiting as a way to influence culture by hiring people that will contribute to a more knowledge-friendly culture [8]. Watch out for incoherent paradigms between personal intents and paradigms of the organization, and use the continuing education of employees as an opportunity to foster knowledge-friendly attitudes and common habits [46].

Understand organizational values

From a knowledge management point of view, the important aspect of organizational culture is the extent to which it is knowledge-friendly. However, cultural change of course requires a much broader focus than that since it is inherently linked to the overall business strategy [56]. Organizational values need to be well understood in order to be able to create an appropriate culture [82].

Culture must not be an excuse

Finally, while culture is of crucial importance, it must not be an excuse for delaying a knowledge management initiative. Do not wait with implementation until you consider the culture to be perfect [124]. In the end, you will want to establish a learning culture. But it may not be needed to start with. Rather, incremental sharing of knowledge itself can often create a learning culture [47].

Lessons Learned about Motivation

Individual motivation is important

Knowledge management usually requires a behavior modification and is often perceived as additional work by employees [41, 111, 46]. In successful knowledge management efforts, participation is generally encouraged but voluntary [118]. Getting people to contribute to and use knowledge management systems is particularly problematic [123]. Role or functional boundaries also tend to inhibit the flow of knowledge [39].

The upshot of all this is that the motivation of employees needs to be carefully considered. Value has to be created not only for the organization as a whole, but also for individuals [82]. That value has to be obvious to employees: Both seekers and providers of knowledge, as well as business managers, must see a positive answer to the old question "What's in it for me?" [151]. This will have to be explained to them in their own terms: Salespeople, for instance, could be motivated by faster close cycles [124].

Incentive and reward systems alone will not be enough to motivate employees, but they may help [143, 161]. Both collective improvement and individual contributions should be rewarded [123]. Knowledge sharing must at least receive appropriate recognition [151].

Incentives can help

Precisely what behaviors should be rewarded will differ from case to case. The most difficult behavior to achieve, and therefore the most obvious candidate for incentives, is generally knowledge sharing [123, 151, 35]. Often, it may also make sense to reward employees for taking the time to seek out and utilize available knowledge [123, 35]. This may go as far as offering small financial incentives for going to the pub for networking purposes [35]. Rewarding teamwork or the use of a knowledge management application has also proven useful in many cases [75, 5].

Decide what to reward

Apart from deciding what to reward, there is the issue of how to reward. Finding effective ways of rewarding employees is not easy at all. In particular, incentives must not be trivial ones such as mouse pads [39]. The most important extrinsic motivators are personal recognition and reputation on the one hand, and compensation and promotion on the other [46]. Financial incentives have shown mixed results in the past; an important point here is that approaches should have a long-term focus, which means linking them to the general evaluation and compensation structure [39, 46].

Effective rewards are difficult

In many cases, the most effective motivators will be intrinsic, such as increases in job efficiency and fun [79]. While such rewards cannot be directly provided, they can be taken into account when designing knowledge management applications.

Lessons Learned about Technology

The first and most important lesson learned about technology is that it can never be a knowledge management solution in itself [123, 59]. A process focus is at least as important as a technology focus [161]. Knowledge management should be problem-driven rather than technology-driven [79]. In many cases, technology cannot replace face-to-face contact [53, 47]. In a sense, knowledge repositories should be regarded

Technology alone cannot deliver KM

as cost centers, since they only capitalize on old ideas, while the real source of wealth is innovation [59].

Technology is important as an enabler

While technology should not be the primary concern of knowledge management projects, it does have an important role to play as an enabler and catalyst [123]. Investments in technology may be regarded as a kind of entry fee: In many cases, little progress will be made without it [151]. Indeed, the technological infrastructure is a major success factor for knowledge management projects [39].

Technology has to address real needs and has to be marketed

Knowledge management systems have to meet the daily needs of their potential users, and the latter have to be aware of that fact—tools do not automatically create their own market, they have to be marketed within the organization [10, 123]. In order to be accepted by employees, knowledge management systems have to offer significant advantages over informal networks [35]. Be wary of systems with built-in assumptions about organizational culture, structure, or work practices [111]. Internal marketing is not only about users, but also about administrators: Internal information technology support, for instance, needs to be kept informed about projects involving external partners [22].

Technology is a matter of pragmatism

Do not make the very costly mistake of trying to immediately build a huge repository for all the knowledge available to your organization [5]. Instead, approach technology in a pragmatic manner: Do not aim for perfection, but rather for getting useful results within a reasonable timeframe [10].

Connect people to information and to people

Use information technology for knowledge management purposes in the obvious way, by connecting people to information that is relevant to them, but also in a more indirect way, by connecting people to other people with the help of information systems [82]. Connecting people with each other is important for two reasons: First, much of the knowledge they possess is tacit and therefore cannot be explicated and stored in a repository. Second, people who do not work side by side typically lack a common perspective; indeed, they may not even be aware of each other's existence. This is a major barrier to knowledge transfer that may be overcome with the help of suitable systems connecting people with each other [123].

Build on existing architectures

Knowledge management tools should be based on existing information and communication architectures [131]. From a technical point of view, this refers to the infrastructure. The danger of some systems becoming data islands can constitute a major barrier [41]. From a user point of view, the need for special software and for climbing the invariably associated learning curve presents a problem. The solution, again, is to build on existing technologies and work through established media like email and the web as much as possible [111].

Information technology can be a valuable help in sorting out existing knowledge and recognizing knowledge gaps [161]. Perhaps the most important reason for trying to leverage existing content, however, is the simple fact that creating quality content is a time-consuming and expensive activity, and any new knowledge management system is usually expected to provide benefits soon [94].

Leverage existing content

As for any other application, ease of use should be a major concern for knowledge management tools [143]. Most systems, even if they do not have a steep learning curve, will take some getting used to until people can use them efficiently. During that time, ease of use and support are especially important in order to prevent people from abandoning the system before they ever start to reap the benefits [111].

Make it easy to use

A requirement particular to knowledge management systems is that they should support informal, natural ways of sharing knowledge with other people [161]. Apart from making the system easier to use, this will also help with gaining acceptance among employees.

Users should be in control of both the content they have contributed and the content that any systems store about them [111]. Being in control of contributed content becomes an issue each time the respective content is displayed to somebody else. For instance, the author may want to be credited as such. On the other hand, in a discussion on a controversial topic, the author may prefer to remain anonymous.

Put users in control

Being in control of content stored about users is particularly important if that content is being used in a way that will occupy the user's time, for instance in the case of yellow pages listings which will lead to colleagues calling for advice on people's areas of expertise.

Miscellaneous Lessons Learned

Since people are always busy and usually do not welcome extra work, knowledge management activities should be embedded as far as possible in work processes that need to be

Embed KM in work processes

carried out anyway and are regarded as a natural part of one's job [123, 56, 111]. This also applies to information technology: Knowledge management components should interface directly with common applications used to carry out that work, for instance word processors [94]. Make capturing insights easier by providing appropriate templates [56].

Knowledge has to be structured

Make knowledge accessible by structuring it [75, 56]. The classification of knowledge is not always easy—difficulties include frequently changing categories and the question of who controls decisions about the structure—but is strongly advised [123, 39, 41]. For navigation purposes, resource maps are particularly useful [161].

Knowledge has to be maintained

Preventing an organizational knowledge base from becoming a useless knowledge junkyard requires investments in knowledge maintenance [124, 75]. This not only includes making sure that relevant knowledge is being kept up to date, but also identifying knowledge that is not relevant any more, but is attracting the attention and wasting the time of employees looking for knowledge that really is relevant to them [35].

Maintaining knowledge, particularly reviewing and editing the content of knowledge management systems, requires experienced practitioners [22]. Enable users of knowledge management systems to point out deficiencies and suggest improvements in a way that keeps the disruption to their flow of work at a minimum. The feedback collected in this fashion will be a valuable help for knowledge maintenance [94].

Pay attention to tacit knowledge

Accord tacit knowledge the attention it deserves [53, 161]. The fact that explicit knowledge is far easier to deal with creates the danger of focusing too much on it to the detriment of the management of tacit knowledge [123].

Establish KM roles

Formalize the roles required for introducing and supporting knowledge management [82]. Process owners, in particular, have to be assigned roles that specify their responsibilities [131]. Furthermore, knowledge champions can be of great help in creating awareness among staff and generally catalyzing the process of introducing knowledge management practices. The role of knowledge champion may be a specially created one, or a role of all leaders [35]. Tutoring and mentoring should also be recognized as knowledge management roles [46]. Establishing new roles will often involve spending money. Nevertheless, some companies have introduced multiple levels of new roles [39]. Often, however, existing roles can be adapted for knowledge management purposes [56].

The success of knowledge management is inevitably tied to the cooperation of people with different backgrounds. In a departmental structure, at least the human resources and information technology departments as well as the strategic level of the organization will have to be involved, and they will need to work together rather than fight about who owns the initiative [10, 5]. If there are negotiations with prospective external partners, lawyers and finance people should also be involved at an early stage [22].

KM requires cooperation

Integrate knowledge management with existing corporate training programs [143]. The introduction of knowledge management systems creates a special need for user training, since this kind of application often goes hand in hand with new work practices [75, 111].

Integrate KM with training

Handling knowledge effectively requires special skills. Staff often lack the necessary expertise, a problem that is aggravated by high employee turnover [41]. Develop the necessary knowledge skills in your organization, especially the skill of adapting knowledge to suit different contexts needs to be developed [35].

Develop knowledge skills

Different channels for knowledge transfer add value in different ways. Offer several such channels. Their synergy will enhance use [39]. Give users a variety of choices and deliver knowledge through the individual's preferred learning channel [82, 35]. In particular, users differ in their preference of push or pull mechanisms and of all-inclusive or selective approaches [161].

Offer multiple channels for knowledge transfer

Do not underestimate the impact of the built environment on knowledge management, particularly its role in fostering or inhibiting ad hoc communication. Take knowledge management issues into account when making decisions about office layout and business locations [46]. This is especially important as virtual organizational forms become more prevalent [35].

Consider the built environment

While generally the big issue is to foster knowledge sharing, be aware that sharing has two major limits. First, there is the issue of confidentiality [124]. Second, privacy issues are becoming more and more important, especially as profiling technologies are increasingly being used [111].

Be aware of limits to knowledge sharing

Focus on the future   Finally, keep in mind that knowledge management is meant to ensure the future competitiveness of one's company—and not to soothe one's conscience about problems experienced in the past. Requirements change. Always focus your knowledge management efforts on issues likely to be important in the future [53]. Creating and sharing just any knowledge will only waste resources; focus on knowledge that will really add value to the company [161].

II

PROCESSES

Chapter 4

Knowledge Planning

Sometimes, by chance, and with a lot of luck, letting chaos reign may actually work. Unless you are willing to stake the future of your organization on that rather slim chance, however, careful planning is imperative for knowledge management.

The lessons learned summarized in chapter 3 have already emphasized the importance of planning in general, and of having a clear knowledge management strategy in particular. This chapter first discusses the setting of knowledge goals, then moves on to the formulation of knowledge management strategies. After that, some common strategies are outlined as examples.

Setting Knowledge Goals

The aim of knowledge planning is to break down a knowledge management initiative into manageable projects, and to do so without losing sight of the big picture [9]. Arguably the most important step in planning a knowledge management program is to set appropriate knowledge goals. Strategies for reaching those goals may be adapted over time. Failure to articulate proper goals, however, will push the whole initiative in a completely wrong direction.

Three types of knowledge goals can be distinguished: Normative, strategic, and operational ones [129]. Normative knowledge goals are about establishing a knowledge-friendly culture as a precondition for the success of other knowledge management measures. Strategic knowledge goals specify

Types of knowledge goals

35

a desirable knowledge portfolio, based on the future knowledge requirements of an organization. The intermediate steps necessary to achieve normative and strategic knowledge goals are the domain of operational knowledge goals.

Required knowledge   The need to properly understand an organization's knowledge requirements has been highlighted by one of the lessons learned. This is particularly important in the context of setting knowledge goals. In fact, it is a precondition for setting knowledge goals that really capture all critical knowledge requirements.

One way to develop a better understanding of a company's knowledge requirements is to consider knowledge from the perspective of its support for a competitive position [178]. First, there is the core knowledge necessary for conducting the particular business the company engages in. Such knowledge merely distinguishes a company from others outside of its own industry, but not from its direct competitors.

Second, there is the advanced knowledge that confers a real competitive advantage. While companies within an industry generally have a similar overall level of advanced knowledge, the specific advanced knowledge held by a company allows it to differentiate itself from the competition.

Third, the kind of innovative knowledge that makes companies industry leaders may in fact permit them to change the rules of the game itself. The important point to keep in mind here is that today's innovations are tomorrow's daily grind. Over time, innovative knowledge will become the core knowledge of the future.

Available knowledge   Moving from the demand side to the supply side of knowledge within an organization, the setting of knowledge goals does not have to be pure guesswork either. While a certain amount of guessing will always be involved, those guesses can at least be turned into educated guesses by surveying what knowledge is already available and how it is, or is not, being used.

Instruments developed for measuring intellectual capital, which are discussed in detail in chapter 10, can give a high-level strategic overview. Relevance feedback collected by systems, either in the form of usage statistics or by having users explicitly rate the relevance of documents, can paint a more detailed picture.

Knowledge goals guide both the formulation of a knowledge management strategy, which is covered in the next section, and the various decisions to be made later on the operational level, for instance when it comes to choosing between different supporting technologies.

Benefits of articulating goals

Furthermore, knowledge goals will typically be used to evaluate the success of the initiative, possibly within a more general framework for measuring intellectual capital, thus closing the cycle of planning, implementing, and assessing.

Beyond those obvious uses, however, the process of deliberately and carefully articulating knowledge goals can also be instrumental in surfacing the expectations of all the people involved, and in reaching a consensus on what to aim for rather than presenting people with faits accomplis. This is important since the success of any large knowledge management project will depend on the commitment of many people with different agendas.

A special case is the preparation of a proposal for a knowledge management project to convince top management of its benefits. In this case, quantifiable knowledge goals that can be used for return on investment calculations will be particularly helpful. This emphasizes the lesson learned about linking knowledge management to business results.

Formulating a Strategy

Once the knowledge goals are set, the challenge is to formulate a knowledge management strategy that sets the course for reaching those goals. The terminology might need some clarification here. A knowledge-based strategy is a general business strategy paying special attention to knowledge aspects. By contrast, a knowledge management strategy is about how to attain knowledge goals.

While the knowledge requirements and the availability of knowledge within the organization should already be fairly clear at this point, further analysis of the status quo is still needed. In particular, existing problems have to be identified, collected, and prioritized in order to be able to decide upon a suitable strategy to overcome them.

Analysis of problems

On the other hand, developing a knowledge management strategy will usually also require an understanding of documented knowledge that goes beyond the content (what is available?) and includes issues of organization and presentation (how is it available?). Criteria for evaluating documents

Analysis of documents

could include language (clarity of writing), logic (flow of arguments), context (relationship to previous research), and organization (emphasis of key messages) [143].

Apart from criteria like these, which characterize the way individual documents look like, attention should also be paid to the way collections of documents are organized. They could, for example, be printed on paper and only accessible through certain people, or they could be electronically accessible by everybody and organized through an elaborate classification scheme.

Analysis of information flows

Information flows should be analyzed too. On the one hand, this concerns documents on their way into, through, and out of the company. On the other hand, information flow analysis also includes project meetings, company events, and any other mechanisms through which information is regularly exchanged, be it verbally, electronically, or on paper.

Adapting strategic analysis tools

Generally, a lot of standard tools for strategic analysis can be adapted to the purpose of formulating a knowledge management strategy. Competitive analysis, environmental scanning, product lifecycle and business portfolio matrices, value chain analysis, scenario planning, and options analysis can all be used with a special focus on knowledge [49].

Another example is gap analysis [178]. Traditional strategic management addresses the gap between what a company should be doing and what it is actually doing. Underlying this strategic gap, there may be a knowledge gap. A knowledge management strategy has to address the closing of this knowledge gap.

The point here is that the knowledge gap is identified not by just any method, but is directly derived from the strategic gap. This makes sure that the knowledge management strategy is aligned with the general business strategy, as demanded by the corresponding lesson learned.

A SWOT analysis (strengths, weaknesses, opportunities, and threats) can also be undertaken in a knowledge-based way [178]. The focus here is on linking knowledge resources and capabilities with their strategic opportunities and threats. Similarly, the strengths and weaknesses associated with the knowledge currently available to the company are identified.

Dimensions to consider

There are a lot of dimensions worth considering when formulating a knowledge management strategy. The four foci of a SWOT analysis are already very useful, but they can still be complemented by a number of others. They all offer different perspectives which ensure that important aspects of a knowledge management strategy will not be overlooked.

First, there is the distinction between what is known (content) and what is known to be known (awareness) [49]. Available knowledge of which the company is aware is the easy part. At worst, some of it may turn out to be of little value for the organization.

Content vs. awareness

Available knowledge of which the company is not aware needs to be identified. Knowledge that is lacking, but with the organization being aware of that lack, calls for a learning strategy. The most difficult case is of course knowledge that is unavailable and not even recognized as such.

Attention also has to be paid to the issue of creating new knowledge versus reusing existing knowledge [178]. While these two strategic foci are not mutually exclusive, the question here is how much effort should go into building up new knowledge domains on the one hand, and leveraging unexploited knowledge on the other. Since the most valuable of all knowledge, strategic knowledge unique to the company, takes a lot of time to develop, a fine balance is needed between the long term and the short term.

Creating vs. reusing

Another dimension concerns the location of the primary sources of knowledge that the company uses. Are they internal or external? Internal knowledge can be of higher strategic value if it is difficult for competitors to obtain or imitate [178]. On the other hand, knowledge from outside sources can introduce fresh ideas and is a sine qua non in the context of benchmarking.

Internal vs. external

There is also a dimension which is not really specific to formulating a knowledge management strategy, but which deserves special mention since it is disregarded all too often. It is the question of urgency versus importance. The problems to be addressed as well as the measures a strategy prescribes as remedies should be examined from this angle. This will help to balance the short term with the long term. Regarding the short term aspects of the strategy, the lessons learned about starting small, conducting a pilot project, and addressing critical business issues right from the start should also be heeded.

Urgency vs. importance

Perhaps the best illustration of the process of formulating a knowledge management strategy appropriate for the needs of a particular organization is to look at four typical stages [84]. First, the overall knowledge management problems have to be defined. This includes establishing the link to the business drivers, relevant processes, types of knowledge that are of interest, sources and users of knowledge, and probable enablers and inhibitors. Suitable templates are a major help in this stage.

Second, the focus of the strategy has to be placed on a manageable set of such problem areas. This involves envisioning the ideal resolution for each problem and establishing priorities. This is also where concrete objectives can be set. It can be helpful to graphically compare the current and the desired future positions along all relevant dimensions.

Third, paths from the status quo to the desired situation have to be identified. This is the first step of moving from the what to the how. For each of the focus areas selected in the previous stage, paths to the resolution of the problems are described in general terms (for example "moving from individually held tacit knowledge to internally shared explicit knowledge").

Last, the knowledge management processes necessary to move along each path have to be identified, along with any organizational factors that might facilitate or inhibit the implementation, down to the finest level of detail that still makes sense for a strategy. Beyond that lies the specific planning for the implementation of the strategy later on, which will rely on the factors identified here.

One final point to remember is the lesson learned about communicating the knowledge management strategy. Ideally, it will be available as a document written in a style appropriate for all staff. Usually a presentation of the knowledge management strategy by top management is also a good idea, as it is not only an opportunity to convey the content of the strategy in a more personal fashion, but also because it demonstrates the commitment of top management to knowledge management.

Common Strategies

The details of any knowledge management strategy will, of course, always be specific to the particular organization concerned. Analysis of companies with knowledge management programs does, however, suggest that most strategies can be meaningfully assigned to one of only a handful of categories sharing similar characteristics. These broad categories often provide valuable guidance in planning one's own knowledge management efforts.

Perhaps the best known of such distinctions is that between codification and personalization strategies [66]. Essentially the same concepts have also been suggested under different names [132].

The basic idea behind a codification strategy is to focus on the efficient reuse of knowledge by making it independent of particular individuals: Connecting people to documents. This kind of strategy is suitable for companies relying on explicit knowledge to offer standardized, mature products. **Codification**

Such companies often hire graduates fresh from college who implement solutions based on the knowledge they find within the company's elaborate databases. Training typically takes place in groups and people are rewarded for using and contributing to knowledge repositories. Heavy information technology investments are made in order to provide an infrastructure facilitating the codification, storage, and dissemination of reusable knowledge. Economically, the aim is to generate large overall revenues.

A personalization strategy, on the other hand, is all about building networks of people and dialogue between individuals, about connecting people to people. This approach is appropriate for companies relying on tacit knowledge to offer highly customized, innovative products. **Personalization**

These companies tend to hire experienced staff, train them through one-on-one mentoring, and reward them for directly sharing knowledge with each other. Information technology plays only a moderate role, usually for facilitating communication and for locating experts on a given topic. The economic focus of this strategy is on maintaining high profit margins.

Naturally, the decision between a codification and a personalization strategy is not an all or nothing affair. Elements of both will usually be found in almost any real enterprise. That is not to say, however, that one should give equal weight to both. Successful companies tend to concentrate their efforts on either codification or personalization [66].

Another helpful framework distinguishes between four generic knowledge management strategies and relates them to the strategic goals of efficiency, innovation, and managing risk [169].

Leveraging

The leveraging strategy focuses on the internal transfer of existing knowledge from various domains. Internal benchmarking may be used to identify promising transfer opportunities.

Efficiency is achieved through sharing knowledge on the operational level. At the same time, the innovation process is improved by sharing knowledge between domains. The strategy contributes to risk management through the sharing of knowledge on competitors and regulatory environments as well as through the reduction of the risk of overtaxing resources.

Expansion

The expansion strategy aims at refining existing knowledge, increasing its scope and depth. Process and product innovations are created by drawing on existing knowledge domains.

This expansion of knowledge about existing processes contributes to efficiency. Risk management is addressed as in the leveraging strategy. In addition, the risk of deterioration of knowledge domains is reduced by developing the knowledge in those domains.

Appropriation

The appropriation strategy, by contrast, is externally oriented. Here, a completely new knowledge domain is built up within the organization by transferring knowledge from outside sources. Hence strategic partnerships and acquisitions will often play an important role.

Efficiency is increased by applying new knowledge transferred from partners on the operational level. Innovation also stands to benefit from the influx of knowledge. The contribution to risk management again lies in reducing the risks of overtaxing resources and of deteriorating knowledge domains as well as in keeping up to date on the external environment.

Probing

Finally, the probing strategy is all about creating new knowledge from scratch. A vision of a future knowledge domain serves as a seed for highly motivated teams to build their own communities and develop both individual and social, both explicit and tacit knowledge.

The aim is, on the one hand, to increase business process efficiency through generating relevant knowledge. On the other hand, it is to foster radical product and process innovation. The main contribution to risk management is to make the deterioration of knowledge domains less likely.

Chapter 5

Creating Knowledge

Many of the approaches discussed under the umbrella of knowledge management are concerned primarily with exploiting existing knowledge. But where does knowledge come from in the first place? This chapter focuses on knowledge creation. That means the development of genuinely new knowledge, as opposed to the more general topic of learning which also includes the absorption of knowledge that already exists elsewhere. The latter is discussed in chapter 6.

First, this chapter sheds some light on the nature of knowledge creation. This includes a brief discussion of related terms, an overview of the best known framework of organizational knowledge creation, and a discussion of important factors influencing knowledge creation. The latter, in particular, should help to identify measures that can be taken on a strategic level in order to create an environment conducive to knowledge creation. The chapter then moves on to methods that can be used to support knowledge creation on the operational level. Finally, various technologies that can support knowledge creation are discussed.

Understanding Knowledge Creation

Knowledge has very different origins in an organization. Apart from the kind of product knowledge that comes out of research departments, there is also process knowledge, which may originate just about anywhere in the organization during everyday work, perhaps even accidentally. Of course, there may also be a department like quality assurance that is

Origins of knowledge

charged with systematically developing such knowledge by analyzing existing processes. The important thing is that the value of both ideas related to products and of new ways of doing things within the organization is recognized.

Creativity

The terms creativity, problem solving, and innovation are closely related to knowledge creation, but do have somewhat different meanings. Creativity can be defined as the mental process of connecting and rearranging of knowledge in order to generate new knowledge [90]. It is therefore an important part of knowledge creation, but does not encompass all of it. It refers only to the flexibility required of the human mind, not to issues of organizational or technological support.

The concept of creativity may be better understood by not considering it as some mystical way of coming up with new and, in some sense, better ideas, but rather as the art of shifting one's perspective in order to see new possibilities relevant to the problem at hand. This can be referred to as "better box thinking" instead of the misleading term "out of the box thinking", taking into account the fact that one always thinks within some box—but that some boxes are better suited for certain problems than others [13].

Problem solving

Problem solving is a more general term, and is related to knowledge creation in so far as a solution found for a problem constitutes new knowledge. Problem solving may be based on insight or on trial and error; creativity may play an important role, but so will analytical thinking.

Innovation

Innovation refers not only to coming up with new ideas, but also to implementing them successfully. Innovation therefore is a broader term than knowledge creation: It is not just about creating knowledge, it is about putting it to use as well.

SECI and "ba"

The most frequently cited framework of knowledge creation in organizations is the one by Nonaka et al. [119, 120]. Knowledge creation, in their view, is the result of a social process between individuals involving the interaction of tacit and explicit knowledge. This leads them to consider four modes of knowledge conversion (SECI) and their resulting types of knowledge: Socialization (from tacit to tacit) creates what they call sympathized knowledge, externalization (from tacit to explicit) results in conceptual knowledge, combination (from explicit to explicit) produces systemic knowledge, and internalization (from explicit to tacit) yields operational knowledge. A distinction is also made between the individual, the group, the organization, and the inter-organizational level. Furthermore, they use the Japanese term "ba" to emphasize the role of the shared context which participants in a knowledge creation process need to interact. This can be a physical, virtual, or mental space.

Factors Influencing Knowledge Creation

An appropriate organizational culture is a precondition for unlocking a company's potential for knowledge creation. Mistakes must be treated as learning opportunities. Employees also have to be given the time necessary for experimenting.

In the end, however, the real bottleneck of knowledge creation is creativity. While this cannot be managed in the strict sense of the word, organizations can establish conditions in which creativity is more likely to thrive. A number of factors influencing creativity have been identified [154].

Creativity is very much about the unexpected, both in terms of what happens (new ideas) and how it happens (the particular situation that sparked an idea). It is therefore important not to impose unnecessary limitations.

> Non-preconception

Many activities which result in the creation of valuable knowledge for the organization begin their lives as unofficial, unanticipated, spontaneous initiatives driven by employee interests. In order to reap the benefits, organizations have to allow and indeed encourage such work with minimal management control.

> Skunk works

Accidental discoveries can be an important source of new knowledge, but only if someone recognizes their potential. Companies can increase the chance for fortunate accidents by encouraging tinkering and experimenting during everyday work, but in order to take advantage of those they also have to increase their sagacity, for instance through job rotation and supporting employees taking courses not related to their current tasks.

> Serendipity

On a related note, employees should have access to a broad range of stimuli not only in special circumstances, but during everyday work. This is best achieved through transcending functional, disciplinary, and organizational boundaries.

> Diverse stimuli

Traditional vertical corporate communication channels often fail to put precisely those employees from different parts of the organization in touch who, based on their work, should

> Internal communication

cooperate optimally from the perspective of knowledge creation. The task for the organization then is to show at least some support for unofficial means of communication, if not to overhaul the entire communication policy.

Reciprocity
Trust has long been recognized as an enabler of knowledge creation. More generally, reciprocity can be key in developing relationships beneficial for creative endeavors, even in competitive environments. Both trust and reciprocity are only effective in situations where individuals expect their contacts to last. It is up to the organization to provide an appropriate environment.

Motivation
Knowledge creation cannot be forced; it relies heavily on intrinsic motivation. To take advantage of this, organizations should try to motivate the direction (but not prescribe the details) of knowledge workers' tasks. Rewards and incentive schemes are a particularly sensitive issue in this context. They are discussed in more detail in chapter 6.

Fun
Finally, one factor that may itself be considered a part of intrinsic motivation deserves special mention: Fun. If knowledge creation is to be fostered, playful behavior needs to be promoted rather than stifled through strict norms with regard to what constitutes "serious" and "professional" behavior [99].

Methods Supporting Knowledge Creation

The factors influencing knowledge creation discussed above should be a valuable help in deciding, on a strategic level, what can be done in a particular organization in order to create an environment fostering and exploiting knowledge creation. Such high-level measures might be establishing research labs or think tanks, cultivating an appropriate attitude towards science and innovation within the organization, conducting innovation management as a formal activity, introducing suggestion schemes, and making sure that team formation is handled appropriately.

However, strategic measures alone will not suffice. Bearing in mind the lesson learned in chapter 3 about the need to develop knowledge skills, the question now is which methods can be used on the operational level to support knowledge creation in everyday work.

Checklists
Helpful methods need not involve any complicated procedures requiring a profound understanding of, say, group

dynamics. They can be as simple as using checklists to ensure that attention is paid to all important aspects of a given problem. Such checklists can range from the "six Ws" (why, where, when, who, what, how) to industry-specific, company-specific, or even customer-specific checklists, for instance for use in new product development.

One can also ask one key question, "Why?", over and over again: The original assumption is questioned, the answer to that is questioned again, etc. After several iterations, the answers can be arranged in some logical order, for example from strategic to operational, resulting in a purpose hierarchy. Each statement can then serve as a starting point for generating a set of alternatives. This may also prove valuable in refocusing the topic.

Purpose hierarchy

Another popular way of encouraging new ideas is to try to imagine how the situation in question might appear to other people with other jobs, children, animals, aliens, or even inanimate objects—anything that might offer a fresh perspective.

Be someone else

Dealing with unexpected stimuli generally encourages creative thinking. The most common way of exploiting this is by taking a random word and trying to find some connection to the topic at hand. For this method, it helps to have pre-selected collections of different kinds of words (nouns, verbs, conjunctions, prepositions). Note that some people find it easier to work with pictures and sounds than with words. When working with analogies, it is important to keep in mind that they do not have to be perfect in order to be useful. Large groups should be split up for this method.

Random stimuli

The process of discovering connections between seemingly unrelated objects is called synectics. The important thing here is to not balk at apparent contradictions, but to instead learn to live with complexity and embrace disruptive thinking with a view to an eventual fusion of opposites.

Synectics

All human thinking is invariably based on many assumptions which usually go unchallenged. In order to encourage creative thinking, however, it often pays to make as many of those assumptions as possible explicit by drawing up a list, and then either drop or even reverse them one by one, or several or all of them at once. Again, any resulting statement that seems nonsensical should be treated as an opportunity for sparking new ideas rather than as an obstacle.

Assumption smashing

Brainstorming

Perhaps the most famous method of knowledge creation in groups is brainstorming. Today, the term is sometimes wrongly used to refer to just about any way of several persons collecting ideas together. The original meaning of brainstorming, however, is characterized by a set of four basic rules. First, there must not be any criticism of ideas during the brainstorming session. Second, quantity is wanted and all ideas are recorded. Third, odd ideas are encouraged. Fourth, combination of and building on ideas voiced by others are welcome.

The importance of properly preparing for a brainstorming session and of documenting and reviewing the results is frequently underestimated. In order to optimally benefit from brainstorming, the problem needs to be clearly stated and understood by all participants. Designated persons should be responsible for enforcing the rules and for documenting all the ideas. The size of the group is also important: With too few people, building on each others ideas will be difficult; with too many people, sessions are difficult to manage and participants might get frustrated because they seldom get to speak.

Brainwriting

Brainwriting refers to a variant of brainstorming in which people write down their ideas instead of talking about them. Several different organized ways of exchanging the documented ideas between participants have been proposed, the idea again being to enable people to build on each others ideas. Brainwriting is particularly helpful as an alternative to classical brainstorming for groups whose conversations tend to be monopolized by one person.

Concept fan

The concept fan is a method for encouraging new ideas about how to carry out processes. Starting with a high-level flowchart of the process as it is currently being performed, one identifies the concepts behind each of the steps and writes them down in a second column to the right of the flowchart. This will often lead to the realization that there are also other ways of achieving those concepts. Such alternatives are documented in a third column to the right of the corresponding concepts.

Morphological approach

The morphological approach is used to come up with novel combinations of alternatives. First, attributes describing the situation are identified. This could, for example, be product parameters that designers can tweak in an engineering setting.

Second, a table is drawn up with a line for each attribute. Each line is filled with all possibilities for the respective attribute that come to mind. Finally, multiple scenarios are generated by choosing different combinations of possibilities for the different attributes. This can be represented graphically by drawing zigzag lines connecting exactly one possibility for each attribute.

Since creative thought works by association rather than in any strictly linear fashion, documenting ideas in a way that preserves as many of those associations as possible often helps to develop new ideas, both through visual feedback on the spot and when revisiting the notes later on. Concept mapping is a popular method for this purpose.

Concept mapping

Different thinking styles can make valuable contributions, but often persons or whole groups are dominated by one or very few styles. This can be overcome by group methods which let participants play different roles, such as "the critic" or "the dreamer". Outward signs, such as differently colored hats, can help people to feel comfortable in their roles without fear of losing face or otherwise perceiving the situation as a threat to their egos.

Thinking hats

Last but not least, dialogue (as opposed to discussion) can be regarded as a valuable approach to creating new knowledge [63]. The guiding principles here are to focus on synergy: Seeking understanding first, and only then being understood; preferring a certain position, but not clinging to it; and generally exploring rather than behaving confrontationally.

Dialogue

Technologies Supporting Knowledge Creation

While knowledge creation is most effectively supported by addressing organizational issues, technology can also make a contribution.

First, since knowledge always builds on previous knowledge, all of the tools that make prior knowledge readily accessible help with knowledge creation as well. Historically, clay, papyrus, paper and ink have been used to write and draw, thus making knowledge available across time and space. Today, electronic repositories feature advanced retrieval techniques that already go far beyond simple full-text searching.

Retrieval tools

In order to optimally support further knowledge creation, however, prior knowledge has to be not only available, but also easily understandable. Diagrams and illustrations have always played an important role and are now being supplemented by video and multimedia. Metadata and annotation technologies further add to the impact of existing information.

Brainstorming tools

More directly related to creating knowledge, electronic brainstorming tools have appeared in a number of forms. They are particularly suited for being used asynchronously, thereby permitting a much larger group of people to be involved than would be possible in a face-to-face setting.

Letting people brainstorm without direct contact to each other and aggregating the results afterwards is called nominal brainstorming, and offers a number of advantages over the traditional method which can be exploited by tools [153]: First, idea entry can be made anonymous, thereby avoiding the problem of participants being reluctant to express their ideas for fear of being judged by their colleagues. Second, a tool's logging capabilities can show the relative performance of individuals in the aggregate and therefore help to reduce free-riding. Finally, all participants can capture their ideas immediately as they occur, without having to wait for another group member to finish with theirs. This eliminates the problem of ideas being forgotten while waiting.

The claim that this kind of software indeed has powerful effects on knowledge creation is also supported by empirical evidence, for instance in the context of issue identification for planning for natural disaster situations [11]. Empirical evidence also suggests that letting subgroups build on the results of previous subgroups, as opposed to letting each subgroup start from scratch, increases not only productivity but also participant satisfaction [42].

Idea processors

More generally, idea processors are a category of software helping users not only with generating and capturing ideas, as in brainstorming applications, but also with organizing and presenting them. For instance, they may guide the user through problem solving exercises, forcing them to think in non-obvious ways. Some idea processors also incorporate components of artificial intelligence [32].

Indeed, the idea to use software to support some further creativity techniques beyond brainstorming seems quite obvious; after all, a lot of knowledge work is conducted in front of the computer screen anyway. Unlike many of the other technologies mentioned here, however, software supporting creativity techniques has so far suffered from a lack of widespread acceptance in many quarters. This may be partly due to the fact that much of it follows unconventional design philosophies and fails to adhere to accepted standards in user interface design, therefore appearing "amateurish" to many "serious" business users. Also, integration with other tools one would typically use in conjunction with creativity software tends not to be a strong point of many of these tools.

Since the most valuable new knowledge is usually created by groups of people rather than by a single person, technologies used to improve the performance of such groups also must be considered. This already begins with the selection of team members, where a healthy mix of competences, professional backgrounds, and personal styles is often crucial for teams expected to come up with new knowledge. Expertise location tools like yellow pages, and technologies to generate them, such as expertise profiling, can be a great help.

Expertise locators

Once a team is selected, different communication technologies ranging from the telephone and email to video conferencing, as well as full-blown groupware environments, enable team members to collaboratively create knowledge even when they are geographically dispersed. In one example, even the use of not much more than email has been found to reduce the complexity of the knowledge creation process [133].

Groupware

Group support systems facilitating face-to-face meetings have also received a lot of attention in the context of knowledge creation [73]. A particularly interesting approach is to employ and extend the metaphor of arranging note cards on a pin board by electronic means using spatial hypertext [125, 78]. Unlike the use of a physical pin board, such an approach could handle several structurally different views of the information fragments being discussed in a workshop simultaneously [135].

Spatial layout of electronic note cards is really just one special case of the much broader domain of information visualization. A host of other visualization techniques, ranging from two-dimensional visualizations of hierarchies and networks to fully immersive three-dimensional virtual realities, can also aid knowledge creation by helping people to discern relationships they would not have noticed in traditional forms of presentation [147]. Concept mapping, already a

Visualization

popular method with pen and paper, also becomes even more powerful when taken into the electronic domain.

Simulations   Another way to discover new relationships is through simulations. The opportunity to play around with things has long been recognized to significantly increase the chances of coming up with novel and useful ideas.

Various kinds of software enable people to do that in different domains and at different levels of abstraction, ranging from the engineer tweaking numerical parameters in a simulation of a particular machine to the mathematician playing around with a set of symbolic equations on a general-purpose computer algebra system, and from the business process reengineering specialist using process modeling tools to the chief executive of a company participating in a high-level business simulation.

Artificial intelligence

Discovering new relationships is not limited to people however. Artificial intelligence technologies are used in data mining and text mining in an effort to automate the process of discovery. More generally, artificial intelligence techniques can be very helpful in generating new ideas, but should never be expected to completely automate their evaluation [15].

On a similar note, it is important to bear in mind that the higher the level of automation is, the more restricted is the domain of discourse of the system. Classical artificial intelligence systems need sets of explicit rules describing the area of application, which can only be reasonably specified for particular, limited domains. Therefore, expectations should not be set too high when it comes to automating knowledge creation in everyday situations.

TRIZ   A hybrid approach employing technology to guide people through problem solving tasks and create new knowledge about possible solutions in the engineering domain is based on the theory of inventive problem solving (TIPS, or TRIZ after its original Russian acronym). The interesting point about this method is that it makes use of a high-level knowledge base assembled through many years of analysis of over two million patents. In terms of level of automation, TRIZ tools thus lie in between the typical uses of visualization and artificial intelligence techniques.

Authoring tools

Finally, it is important to realize that in most cases, knowledge that has just been created by people thinking and talking will not be documented with the help of tools specifically tailored to that purpose, such as brainstorming software, but rather by using authoring tools with a more general focus. Since a lot of valuable knowledge can get lost in the process, these tools are important to the overall impact of knowledge creation endeavors.

However, even most full-blown authoring solutions today are essentially not much more than glorified word processors. Large aircraft manufacturers use sophisticated systems for their technical documentation and there is much talk about the semantic web, but on the whole, the use of the kind of structured authoring that would actually facilitate knowledge creation on a large scale is still hardly developed. Ontology editors, for instance, tend not to be suitable for non-specialist users.

Chapter 6

Integrating Knowledge

The previous chapter has focused on the creation of new knowledge. This chapter is about making existing knowledge available to an organization. First, ways of acquiring knowledge from external sources are considered, such as hiring and training staff, cooperating with other organizations, and buying knowledge products. After that, the chapter moves on to knowledge that already exists within the company in some form, but is in danger of getting lost or is simply not accessible to all who would benefit from it, particularly if it is locked away in the heads of some employees. The task of discovering knowledge that has not previously been recognized as such in corporate repositories is also discussed. Finally, the role of incentive schemes for integrating knowledge is considered.

Integrating External Knowledge

Knowledge will always flow across company boundaries. Of interest here in the context of integrating external knowledge are inbound knowledge flows: All the ways in which organizations can gain access to knowledge they need from external sources.

One way to make external knowledge available within an organization is to acquire knowledge products. This includes buying knowledge in the form of research reports or market analyses, and licensing the content of commercial databases, delivered either on CD-ROM or through an online subscription.

Knowledge products

Software products embody knowledge as well. Patents can be licensed or acquired. There are also many knowledge products that do not come with a hefty price tag attached: The amount of knowledge that may be gathered from open sources, either on the world wide web or through more traditional channels such as government offices, is often underestimated.

 Information technology generally plays a vital role in dealing with knowledge products. First, the identification of knowledge products worth buying will often happen through online searching. Second, the delivery of the product will usually involve information technology in one form or another, even if the product itself is delivered on paper. Third, with more and more knowledge products being distributed electronically rather than printed on paper, the use of those products will also depend on appropriate technology.

Finally, beyond the immediate use of the product for the purpose which motivated the decision to buy, knowledge products should not only be kept accessible, but should be kept accessible in a way that enables potential users to actually find them. In other words, they should become part of a corporate repository and be indexed, which again requires suitable technologies. Document management systems enable companies to store, organize, and retrieve diverse collections of documents in a consistent manner. These systems are discussed in chapter 14.

Training and recruiting staff Taking a longer term focus, staff may acquire knowledge available elsewhere through various training activities like attending seminars and workshops, but also through eLearning. Hiring new staff can also be regarded as an instrument for integrating knowledge into the company.

Skills management Both training and hiring benefit from skills management systems. In the case of training, these systems help with planning who should best attend which courses with a view to their current jobs, but also in the context of succession planning. For recruiting, skills management systems not only streamline the efficiency of the process, but also increase its effectiveness: Used properly, they can often provide a more reliable guide to what competences are available or lacking in an organization than managers' gut feeling [61].

Communities of practice Communities of practice, groups of people who do the same things, often transcend organizational boundaries [174].

Engineers, for example, communicate with their peers both within and outside the company. Communication within such communities is frequently more efficient than formal channels for getting at knowledge. Participating in communities of practice therefore offers a great opportunity for integrating external knowledge.

Even former employees can be a valuable source of knowledge. If they part in good understanding, chances are they will become valuable additions to the organization's network of contacts who can be called upon when particular questions arise. Furthermore, one should not forget the possibility that one day they might come back. Creating and supporting corporate alumni networks, for example by providing a website which helps them with their networking, may be a key to leveraging the knowledge of former employees.

Former employees

Another option for getting at knowledge is through consultants, who will analyze the issues confronting the client company without being set in the ways of that company. They will find it easier to see things from a fresh angle and contribute appropriate knowledge.

Consultants

Close cooperation with other companies along the supply chain also opens up ample opportunities for gaining access to valuable knowledge. Much can be learned from other companies operating in the same industry too, from partners as well as through competitive intelligence. Finally, companies can tap the knowledge of universities and non-university research institutions.

Cooperation

There are many options for the degree of cooperation between organizations, ranging from occasional information and cooperation to strategic networks, joint ventures, minority or majority holdings, and outright takeovers and mergers. The amount of knowledge becoming available increases along this continuum, but so does the necessary investment [128].

To sum up, the task of integrating external knowledge may be regarded as a question of deliberately managing the relationships with and use of various sources of knowledge outside the organization.

Integrating Internal Knowledge

In any organization, a lot of knowledge already exists in some form but is not really available to all who would benefit from it. Some knowledge may also be present only temporarily and be lost again unless steps are taken to preserve it. Furthermore, people may not even be aware of the existence of much of the knowledge hidden in an organization. Integrating internal knowledge refers to the task of making all these kinds of knowledge available to whoever needs them within the organization.

What to capture   Since knowledge is being used all the time by employees in their daily work, an obvious approach would be to try to capture as much of that knowledge as possible as it is used, in a non-obtrusive way. There are two problems with this approach. First, drawing the line between what is too obtrusive and what is not is notoriously difficult. Second, even if some knowledge can be captured easily, this does not necessarily imply that it should be.

Instead, the knowledge management strategy should identify which kinds of knowledge are the most valuable ones for a company. Rather than trying to capture everything and ending up with a huge but mostly useless repository, which after all will also need to be administrated, the focus can then be on selectively capturing only knowledge of particular value to the company.

Capturing   Context is an essential aspect of knowledge. One should
context   therefore strive to capture information about the situation in which the capturing took place along with the knowledge itself. A significant part of this may be achieved automatically.

An insurance claims processing employee documenting a decision for future reference, for example, should not have to explicitly write down factors that can easily be deduced from the existence of previous correspondence, internal documents, and the workflow enacted. Document management and workflow management systems may provide this kind of information and could therefore be used to automatically capture at least some of the relevant context.

When to capture   In this example, it is fairly obvious that this kind of knowledge is best captured on the spot. In general, however, questions about the optimal time to capture a given type of knowledge often arise. Some knowledge may need to be made available to the organization in real time, while other cases are not that time-critical.

Apart from the question of when the knowledge is going to be needed by the organization, one also should consider the fact that the human memory is not always a reliable guide to what actually happened. Perceptions often change over time.

After action reviews are a case in point if they are not conducted immediately after the events in question. At the end of a project, for instance, team members are often asked what expectations they had of the project, and to what extent those expectations have been met. It might be wiser to document their expectations at the beginning of the project, and to systematically collect feedback continuously throughout the project rather than just at the end.

Another question that may prove critical to the success of an attempt to capture knowledge, particularly from experts with a high workload, is who to involve to what extent. Expecting experts to spend much of their working time writing reports of the "I am currently working on ..." variety is not very realistic in most cases. At least up to a point, however, other staff may be able to write reports along the lines of "Dr. Smith is currently working on ...".

Who to involve

One of the lessons learned in chapter 3 has been to embed knowledge management in work processes as far as possible. The way in which knowledge is going to be captured, therefore, should be designed in a way that will not be perceived as a distinct task, but as a natural part of one's work. In many cases, information technology can contribute to make this happen.

How to capture

As a simple example, consider an employee writing a letter to a researcher at a university, requesting information on a certain topic. The employee will have to include the address of that researcher and a brief description of the topic. Now a system could capture the facts that that researcher is an expert on that topic, and that that employee has had contact with him, without any significant additional effort on the part of the employee.

Most approaches to capturing knowledge presuppose that the employees concerned are in fact capable and willing to share their knowledge. Very often, however, this cannot be taken for granted.

For the purposes of integration, knowledge has to be shared in a way that makes that knowledge available to the organization at large. This usually means that the knowledge in question has to be explicated in some form. Often, this is more difficult than one might think. Explicating knowledge

Capability to share

properly requires substantial skills on the part of the employees who are expected to share their knowledge. It is therefore important to first make sure that those employees are actually up to the job.

Aiding knowledge explication

Information technology may be of some help in this regard. For one thing, it may be the medium of choice to provide employees with templates and other materials which aid them in finding an effective way of explicating their knowledge. In principle, such means could, of course, also be paper-based.

Where information technology truly comes into its own, however, is not so much in providing static templates but rather in dynamically assisting users in their attempts to explicate knowledge. A simple example for this might be a user typing away, and the system responding with a question in order to clarify the meaning of an ambiguous word. This does not require anything more sophisticated than a thesaurus. As ever more powerful technologies dealing with the semantic level of language become available, we can expect to see much more advanced tools aiding interactive knowledge explication in the future.

Willingness to share

Once employees' ability to share their knowledge is ensured, it is their willingness to actually do so that takes center stage. Unless a culture that favors this kind of behavior is already in place, this may well be the most difficult issue of all. It is certainly to be found at the top end of the most frequently cited problems in knowledge management.

Trust

Trust plays a major role in this context, as one of the lessons learned has pointed out. There is potential for a virtuous circle here: Trust enables knowledge sharing, and frequent sharing of knowledge in turn increases transparency and fosters trust among employees.

"Knowledge is power"

The real problem with the attitude "knowledge is power" can be a very fundamental one: In some organizations, even in ones preaching the value of sharing knowledge, this attitude still accurately reflects the actual situation. The only sustainable way out for the organization is to reduce conflicts of interest between its goals and those of its employees. This may require changes in both formal and informal structures. Companies need to offer their employees a perspective which does not give rise to such a conflict of interests. Only then a culture that is friendly towards knowledge sharing can develop.

Avoiding such conflicts of interests is a necessary precondition for knowledge sharing, but it may not be sufficient. While not being a panacea or applicable to all organizations, incentive schemes have proven useful in the past for motivating employees to share their knowledge with others.

Indeed, incentives are relevant not only to knowledge sharing, but also to other aspects of integrating knowledge, such as overcoming the not-invented-here syndrome by getting employees to look for and integrate knowledge available outside the company. Therefore, incentives are discussed in more detail in a section of their own at the end of this chapter.

Any attempts to find generally applicable approaches to solving the puzzle of how to best motivate employees to share their knowledge are bound to be fruitless. What can always be done, however, is to be very careful not to needlessly exacerbate the problem by demotivating employees, for instance by specifying work processes that are not aligned with knowledge management goals or by introducing systems with cumbersome user interfaces.

What sometimes tends to be forgotten among all the talk about the cultural issues around knowledge sharing is that in order to actually share knowledge, employees not only need the capability and the willingness to do so, but also the opportunity. Sharing knowledge takes time. Employees need to have that time, and they also have to perceive it that way.

In practice, for management this usually translates to "employees need to be given that time". Managers paying lip service to knowledge management and intoning its slogans about sharing knowledge, but failing to create an organizational environment which actually gives employees the opportunity to share, will only lead to frustration all around.

Both capturing and sharing knowledge presuppose that people are aware of the existence of that knowledge. So what about the knowledge that may be hidden in all the various documents, databases, and other information systems in a company? Here the task is to identify knowledge that has not be recognized as such through analyzing existing collections of data and the relationships between them.

Manually sorting through vast amounts of data is out the question. On the other hand, systems, left to themselves, will

Incentives

Not aggravating the problem

Opportunity to share

Identifying knowledge

rarely be able to come up with precisely the kind of analysis that proves useful for people. After all, systems are generally incapable of really understanding the context of the subject matter being analyzed and of the tasks the analysis is intended to support.

Usually, one will therefore opt for a semiautomatic approach which relies heavily on information technology but also involves human judgment at crucial steps. This leads to an iterative process with feedback loops, and the role of the people involved is to direct that process.

KDD and data mining

The technologies used for analysis purposes employ advanced statistical or linguistic methods, even artificial intelligence techniques. Knowledge discovery in databases (KDD) and data mining are particularly pertinent in this context. The two can be distinguished by regarding KDD as the overall process of turning low-level data into knowledge, and data mining as just one step in that process, namely the extraction of patterns or models from observed data [60].

Data mining vs. text mining

Identifying knowledge therefore often relies on data mining, but goes beyond it not only because it encompasses more steps, but also because data mining typically deals with huge amounts of data collected in a data warehouse, whereas knowledge may also be identified in comparatively small collections of text documents. The distinction between analyzing huge amounts of numbers like sales data of a chain of retail stores, and analyzing text documents like project reports of a consultancy, is sometimes made by referring to the former as data mining and to the latter as text mining.

A prerequisite for this kind of knowledge identification is that all relevant data be gathered together from various sources, including not only databases and the company intranet, but also removable electronic media like floppy disks, CD-ROMs, and backup tapes, as well as paper documents that may have to be scanned and converted into text files.

Visualization

Another way in which information technology can help people identify knowledge is through advanced visualization methods. Provided the information is presented in an appropriate fashion, the human perceptual system can detect many kinds of patterns in large collections of information not only at a much higher rate than human cognitive abilities permit when processing written texts, but also at a higher rate than even the best computer systems.

Visualization systems for knowledge discovery purposes available today make a point of supporting two-way interaction with users. Facilities are also provided to allow users to visualize the development of themes over time, which can be a particularly helpful in identifying relationships [160].

And what about identifying the knowledge hidden in the heads of people? This is a much tougher order, and will require a lot of further research. It lies in the nature of this task that it can only be approached indirectly; were it possible to directly identify such knowledge, it would not be hidden in the first place.

Identifying expertise

While much work remains to be done in this area, two ways of approaching the problem can already be made out. First, with a people focus, initiatives to measure intellectual capital may uncover the existence of such knowledge through the use of appropriate indicators (see also chapter 10).

With a technology focus, systems going beyond the usual analysis of documents could also infer expertise in certain areas. For example, even if someone has never authored a document on a certain subject, and is never mentioned in such documents, the fact that this person constantly receives requests for help by email may point to the fact that he has special knowledge in that area.

Incentive Schemes

Integrating external knowledge requires employees who do not suffer from the not-invented-here syndrome and are willing to look for answers not only within their organization, but also outside. Integrating internal knowledge requires employees to be willing to share their knowledge with others. And while the amount of additional work necessary for capturing knowledge should be minimized, it will often still be significant. In short, integrating knowledge stands to benefit hugely from incentive schemes.

Why incentives?

This is not to say that incentives are always necessary or even a good idea. Some organizations may not need them at all, and even among organizations where they do make sense, there are cases in which incentive schemes have completely failed [39]. Moreover, the need for incentives may be lessened by taking appropriate steps earlier on, for instance by trying to hire the kind of people who will contribute knowledge naturally anyway.

In practice, however, organizations often reward counterproductive behaviors like knowledge hoarding while failing to reward productive behaviors like knowledge sharing, and further undermine employees' long-term commitment and a sense of common purpose by excessive downsizing and outsourcing [7]. Such organizations' incentive and reward systems are therefore due for an overhaul from a knowledge management perspective.

Types of incentives

Different incentives address intrinsic motivators like human contact, meaning, self-realization, or any others that are inherent in activities themselves, and extrinsic motivators like money, security, and prestige.

Extrinsic motivators

Incentives increasing extrinsic motivation are generally easier to manage and include performance premiums, pay raises, pensions, and status symbols like office space and reserved parking lots. In one company, for example, cash incentives were given to employees for filing patent applications, regardless of their success, in an effort to increase knowledge sharing [69]. A particularly interesting option is to reward employees with time: The time for a sabbatical, the time for a postgraduate degree, or simply a percentage of working time at the employees' own disposal [122].

Intrinsic motivators

Opportunities to learn through challenging work assignments and through working with renowned experts are good examples for incentives based on intrinsic motivation. Other possibilities in this category include constant feedback by coaches or mentors and attractive job rotation schemes which avoid too narrow specialization.

When it comes to sharing and using knowledge, intrinsic motivation is usually much more important than extrinsic motivation [122]. In fact, it will often be practically impossible to measure individual contributions to some of the most important parts of a company's knowledge. In that case, incentives schemes relying solely on extrinsic motivators make little sense. Incentives addressing intrinsic motivation, by contrast, lose none of their power.

Credits for uploads

In the context of knowledge repositories, one possible approach consists of rewarding all contributions with credits, which are in turn necessary in order to retrieve content contributed by others from the repository. In order for this to work, contributions will have to be valued higher than retrievals. While all contributions should be acknowledged, they will have to be filtered without being overly selective. This will require a fair amount of human judgment [7].

Taking only the amount of knowledge shared into account generally does not provide a particularly good estimate of the value of that knowledge, since it neglects the quality and the usefulness of the knowledge in question. A more general approach is to tie incentives to knowledge objectives [122].

Companies which already practice management by objectives will find it particularly easy to add individual objectives related to sharing and using knowledge and use those as a basis for rewards. The extent to which knowledge objectives have been met by individual employees, as well as other estimates of employees' contributions to integrating knowledge, can be assessed in the course of ongoing personnel evaluation, for instance through periodic talks with each employee.

Incentive systems focused too narrowly on individual performance can be a major barrier on the way to knowledge sharing between individuals [122]. The key here lies in tying incentives to goals that employees can influence but not achieve on their own [69]. The easiest form of this is to offer rewards that depend on the performance of a group, a division, or the whole company.

While the idea behind incentive schemes in the context of knowledge management generally is to foster knowledge sharing behaviors, the reason behind introducing one may also be the wish to communicate knowledge management attitudes to employees. For this purpose, playful approaches involving points and gadgets will be perfectly justified, although they will hardly be as effective as bigger and more formal incentive schemes with regard to directly increasing knowledge sharing.

Finally, it is important to realize that the introduction of incentives will rarely have an instant effect. Over time, however, they do help to accelerate behavioral change [43]. Empirical evidence also shows that successful companies tend to have broad incentive systems which include knowledge management criteria [69].

Margin notes:

Using knowledge objectives

Rewarding groups instead of individuals

Communicating attitudes

Chapter 7

Organizing Knowledge

The previous two chapters have dealt with the creation of new knowledge and with making existing knowledge accessible to a company. In order to really contribute to value creation, however, knowledge has to be not only present and accessible, but also organized in an appropriate fashion.

This chapter first reviews the benefits of organizing knowledge properly. An overview of the kinds of structures typically used to organize knowledge and some examples of knowledge organization in different contexts follow. After that, aspects to be considered when implementing a project with the aim of organizing knowledge are discussed. Finally, the question of who should be responsible for the tasks involved is addressed.

Benefits of Organizing Knowledge

Why is it so important to organize knowledge properly? The most common argument is to increase the efficiency and effectiveness of retrieving knowledge when it is needed: To find only relevant knowledge, and to find all relevant knowledge.

Retrieving knowledge

Browsing through a large amount of content, perhaps not yet knowing precisely what one is looking for, generally requires some kind of navigation through categories. The task of organizing knowledge, then, is to supply a suitable set of categories and to assign documents to them.

When it is clear from the outset exactly which knowledge is being sought, direct searching for keywords is of course possible and does not require any sophisticated organization of the knowledge in question. Still, subject categories and other metadata often are a valuable help in this case, too.

Displaying context

Beyond retrieval, when one is already working with some piece of knowledge, the categories established by knowledge organization can give an indication of the context around the current focus. Both the subject headings a document is associated with and a list of other documents within the same categories can be used for that purpose.

Gaining an overview

On a higher level, the classifications and knowledge maps typically resulting from the process of organizing knowledge are often the best way to gain an initial overview of what knowledge is available at all, and of how different domains relate to each other.

Intelligent processing

If organizing knowledge is taken as far as formalizing knowledge to the point where it is suitable for automated processing not just of documents describing that knowledge, but also of the semantics of those documents, then artificial intelligence techniques can be employed for automated reasoning based on that formalized knowledge.

Interviews with experts, for instance, will usually be documented in textual form. Now the resulting documents can be assigned some subject headings in order to aid their retrieval later on. Formalizing that knowledge, however, would mean investing much more effort, building a full-blown ontology for the subject domain which could then act as a knowledge base for an expert system.

Facilitating communication

Last but by no means least, organizing knowledge in a coherent fashion and making the resulting scheme available to all interested parties will often facilitate communication between those parties.

The use of controlled vocabularies ensures that people know what others are talking about. Structures like classification schemes and knowledge maps tailored to the needs of a particular company aid communication, too, by building a shared perspective, a common understanding. Whether they are aware of it or not, people always have mental maps of the knowledge they are concerned with. These structures may become shared mental maps.

Types of Structures

Term lists

The simplest types of structures used for organizing knowledge are just lists of terms like glossaries and dictionaries. Lists of geographical features are also called gazetteers. Authority files are term lists that single out preferred terms among groups of equivalent terms.

One particular kind of a controlled vocabulary is a thesaurus, which usually lists not only equivalent terms (synonyms), but also shows hierarchical relationships by listing broader and narrower terms. Related terms associated with an entry are generally provided as well. While there are thesauri with a very broad focus, such as the English language in general, most of them have been developed for particular domains of knowledge, for instance fields of science or technology. **Thesauri**

Semantic networks can exhibit even more structure. They often deal with relationships of a broad range of types, including for instance causal relationships. Some semantic networks derived from the automated analysis of large bodies of text also include affinity metrics describing the relative strength of the connections between the terms. **Semantic networks**

Such metrics naturally depend on the domain in which they are used. For example, possible causes linked to the term "accident" might include "force majeure" and "speeding". In the context of a car insurance company, however, the latter is likely to carry more weight.

Probably the most widely used structures for organizing knowledge today are classification schemes, also referred to as taxonomies or categorization schemes. Typical classification schemes consist of a hierarchy of categories successively splitting up the subject domain into ever smaller subdomains. **Classification schemes**

Some of the large and sophisticated classification schemes used by libraries today have taken more than a century to evolve into their present form. These schemes include not only deep hierarchies intended to cover all aspects of human knowledge, but also detailed descriptions of the rules and of the overall philosophy behind the structure.

At the other end of the spectrum, a multitude of small home-grown classification schemes are used on a daily basis for comparatively simple ways of organizing knowledge—just think of the folder structure on your computer's hard drive.

Hierarchical classification schemes are subject to a number of challenges, including the their need to make major philosophical assumptions about the subject domain, but also the very practical issue of lacking flexibility: Trying to keep a large hierarchical classification scheme up to date with changing user needs, but at the same time keeping it internally consistent, can be a nightmare.

Faceted classification, also called analytico-synthetic classification, aims to address such concerns by defining mutually exclusive and collectively exhaustive facets of a subject, and using a combination of those rather than a place in a hierarchy to specify categories. Facets could, for example, include actions, space, and time. In this simple example, one could easily construct a category for wars in 17th century Europe without having to know much about any overall structure.

In terms of information processing, faceted classification can be thought of as assigning attributes for carefully chosen dimensions to each object in a collection. Retrieval then becomes filtering with the help of those metadata.

Subject headings

In addition to a classification scheme, libraries often use subject headings. These are typically less structured than the classification scheme, with only a shallow hierarchy, the emphasis being on the breadth of scope and on the rules for joining subject headings in order to describe an object.

Ontologies

The term ontology, although sometimes misused for simpler structures, really refers to the most formal and explicit abstract models used for organizing knowledge, originally coming from the field of artificial intelligence. Ontologies are machine readable and include definitions for both the types of concepts used and for any constraints on their use [14].

Being able to express complex relationships and rules, ontologies help to create a shared understanding between people, between systems, and between people and systems. With the help of ontologies, software can perform automated reasoning. The semantic web and semantic web enabled services, for instance, are based on ontologies.

The effort required to develop an ontology, however, is generally very high. Most importantly, although ontologies are a very powerful instrument for their domain of application, useful ontologies have only been developed for relatively limited domains so far. An ontology encompassing the range of subjects addressed by common classification schemes is still far on the horizon.

In any discussion of structures for organizing knowledge, knowledge maps deserve a special mention. This is really an umbrella term covering just about any kind of structure that may be visualized in two dimensions, for instance tables and concept maps.

Knowledge maps

Precisely what is depicted in a knowledge map also varies with the particular purpose of the map. It could be items of knowledge, but also knowledge sources (both people and repositories), locations, activities, flows, and applications. Unlike with most other structures for organizing knowledge, care is generally taken with knowledge maps to make them visually appealing. The general idea is to give a high-level overview, usually for non-specialists.

Most of the structures used for organizing knowledge in practice are of a static nature. This raises the question whether dynamic structures, which constantly adapt themselves to users' needs and current work contexts, should not receive more attention. The answer is yes, they should. A lot of further research is needed.

Dynamic structures

It is important to realize that this is not just a question of technology. While the technical issues involved, such as machine learning, are certainly challenging, there are also psychological factors to be considered.

In particular, the familiarity of a structure is lost to the user if that structure is constantly changing. The benefits of dynamic structures may outweigh this drawback in a typical research setting, but when the knowledge domain is relatively well understood, safety is critical, and time is short—think of documentation used in an emergency in a nuclear power plant—one just does not want people wondering "Now where did that category go?"

Some Examples

The most obvious examples of collections to be organized are of course large numbers of documents, be they electronic ones on a corporate intranet or books in a library. In order to get a better idea of the scope of the whole process, however, here are some further examples.

How do people organize all the email they get? Their options are, of course, constrained by the features offered by the software they use. Most email clients, however, allow the user to create a folder hierarchy for archiving messages.

Personal email

In addition, users can usually specify explicit rules which the client then uses to automatically sort incoming messages into those folders. Since formulating such rules is often not exactly easy, some advanced clients provide more intelligent functionality, for instance by suggesting an appropriate folder for each incoming message, and also explaining why that folder is deemed appropriate by the system [38].

A study on how managers actually classify business-related email revealed four major influences [108]. The first reflects the immediate needs of managers, with messages being grouped primarily by content: What the managers themselves must do, what others must do, as well as items of interest without associated actions. The second constitutes the use of the inbox as a kind of crude task manager. The third focuses on scanning the environment: What are other people in the organization doing? Finally, messages are classified according to the perceived future need of the knowledge contained in them.

Discussion list archives

Organizing personal email can already be quite a challenge. So what about the archives of email distribution lists or web-based discussion forums? By far the most common way of organizing such messages is by constructing a hierarchy out of the chronological order in which new topics were introduced, and of who replied to whom within each topic. Nevertheless, more complex ways of organizing them have also been explored, including faceted classification [96].

Websites

With so much knowledge being made available through websites, the general design of their navigation facilities becomes an important focus for organizing knowledge. Hyperlinks are of course the most obvious mechanism used here, either in a constrained fashion through hierarchical menus, or as links occurring in the body of the text, which collectively form a network of directed connections. With links being placed manually and without constraints, link management becomes an important issue in order to avoid links whose targets have long ceased to exist.

There is also another mechanism at work here which deserves more attention than is often being paid in practice: It is the way web page addresses are constructed. Users often take that as a hint when navigating large sites, and while complex structures of course cannot be depicted well by purely hierarchical schemes, structures are often needlessly obscured by using addresses consisting, for instance, mainly of long unintelligible numbers.

It will hardly come as a surprise that particular ways of organizing knowledge have been developed for special purposes. For example, there is software that helps to organize the process knowledge involved in goal oriented decision making [12].

Special applications

The point here is not to come up with completely new structures that nobody has ever thought of before. Rather, the challenge lies in deciding which structure is the most appropriate one for which task, and then providing such a structure along with an interface that is suitable for the intended user group.

Classification schemes and similar structures obviously are a very powerful instrument for organizing documented knowledge, but to what extent do they help to organize all the knowledge people carry around in their heads?

Mental maps

One cannot simply impose some new structure on human memory. People construct their own mental maps, and strong ties in the mind will only be established with topics one can relate to in some significant way in the light of one's own unique history of experiences.

Yet structures encountered repeatedly do shape people's memory and thinking. Also, the human brain absorbs some kinds of structures more easily than others. Structures used for organizing documented knowledge thus can be expected to have an effect on knowledge organization within the brain. It is important to realize that this is a double-edged sword: Being very proficient in thinking along the lines of one structure will often also mean finding it harder to see things from a different perspective.

Finally, how does one gain an overview of all the knowledge available of a particular kind, from a particular set of sources, for a particular group of people, or supporting a particular task? The most popular answer to this question are knowledge maps. Other structures that do not place as much emphasis on visual presentation may also be explored, such as yellow pages which list the areas of expertise of employees.

The big picture

Ideally, there will be a knowledge map providing a high-level overview specifically for the task at hand, and it will be electronically linked to more detailed structures like controlled vocabularies and yellow pages enabling users to zero in on their subject of interest.

Implementing Knowledge Organization

Analyzing user needs

How does one go about organizing knowledge? The general thrust of the initiative should be clear from knowledge planning, as discussed in chapter 4. A more detailed analysis of user needs—precisely which content and which functionality users will need to accomplish knowledge goals—is still required in most cases. This is especially important for large-scale projects, where choosing an inappropriate structure is a very expensive mistake: It takes a lot of effort to reorganize everything all over again.

Using existing structures

The basic choice to be made is between using an existing structure or developing a new one from scratch. One advantage of adopting existing structures is of course that it is generally not as expensive and time-consuming as building one's own. Perhaps more important, however, is the fact that structures for organizing knowledge benefit from having been developed over time: They may appear more trustworthy than home-grown solutions [76].

Structures worth considering that have been published include library classification schemes, Internet directories, and industry specific standards. Such structures can of course be directly adopted as they are. More often, however, they will be adapted to the particular requirements of the organization.

Developing new structures

When developing a structure tailored to the company's needs, it may be helpful to carefully consider a representative sample of items not just in terms of their subject, but also along a broad range of dimensions describing their context, such as time, place, persons, departments, roles, activities, projects, and events.

The results of a more general knowledge assessment, as discussed in chapter 10, may also suggest aspects that should be taken into account when designing a structure to organize that knowledge.

For example, the assessment may reveal that there is an increasing emphasis on obtaining knowledge from suppliers. In that case, one would have a closer look at the way those suppliers structure their knowledge. The new knowledge structure being developed may then reflect the suppliers' approaches, thereby reducing the effort required later to associate content with the structure.

In some cases it makes sense to support several different structures simultaneously. This obviously applies to the transition period when moving from an old scheme to a new one, or when integrating collections. Unless one intends to reclassify everything according to the new scheme from scratch, the challenge here lies in mapping one structure onto the other, comparability and compatibility being notoriously difficult to achieve [148].

Using multiple structures

Another context in which the parallel use of two structures suggests itself is when a lot of content already comes in structured form from external sources, for instance tagged according to the Library of Congress classification scheme. In that case, the company might decide to keep that useful information, but also establish a custom set of keywords that is more detailed in the company's field of operation.

Once a structure is established, pieces of content have to be associated with elements of that structure. This could, for example, mean filing documents into appropriate places of a folder hierarchy. It could equally well mean editing records in a database describing resources only available on paper and assigning subject headings to them, as in traditional libraries. The key question here is to what extent this process can be automated.

Tagging content

Automated approaches to both segmentation (generating categories) and classification (associating documents with categories) promise to be much cheaper, and also much faster, than manual approaches for large collections. The accuracy achieved cannot compare with the work performed by professionals, however, and the initial investments may still be substantial.

Manual vs. automated approaches

Apart from producing results of a higher quality, manual approaches also have the advantage of providing associations that can be explained. If a user does not understand the reasoning behind an association or questions its validity, there is always a person somewhere who can explain that association. Many of the systems proposed to automate the process are not able to give explanations in terms people can easily understand.

In the end, the decision between manual and automated approaches will have to balance the accuracy required with the costs entailed by the various solutions. Hybrid approaches often emerge as a sensible compromise. Automated systems can provide good guesses, which professionals then only have to review rather than work out all on their own.

Introducing new structures

If all authors of documents are expected to take part in associating documents with a structure, for instance by assigning keywords to them using a controlled vocabulary or by classifying them according to a particular scheme, then care has to be taken to make those employees aware not only of the existence of the newly established structure, but also of the precise meanings of its elements.

On the other hand, systems employing structures for organizing knowledge may also operate transparently, without requiring the user to know much about them. A search engine for document retrieval, for instance, may use a thesaurus behind the scenes.

Just providing an effective and efficient way of structuring knowledge is not enough, however. The whole exercise will be nothing but a waste of resources unless it is also accepted by its intended users. If no consistent structure has been available so far, users will generally be grateful, provided the initiative does not result in a significant amount of additional work for them.

If, on the other hand, some structure has already been well established for a long time and enjoys high acceptance, it is critical to communicate the benefits that the new structure will have over the current one for the individual user. Underestimating employees' attachment to entrenched ways of working in general, and of organizing knowledge in particular, can be a very costly mistake.

Visualizing structures

The power of structures lies in their ability to provide orientation and meaning to the user. This can only be accomplished through an appropriate user interface. Both information professionals developing a structure and end users browsing it benefit from a visualization which depicts the relations of various elements.

In particular, users get a far better feeling for the overall structure than through a user interface which only displays one element at a time, with associated ones only accessible through textual links. The spectrum of visual languages that can be employed covers a wide range from the informal to the very formal and constrained [92].

Finally, it is important to realize that organizing knowledge is not a one-off event. Both the structures and the associations between them and items of content need to be maintained. This is discussed in detail together with other aspects of maintaining knowledge in chapter 9.

Maintaining structures

Responsibilities for Organizing Knowledge

Whose responsibility should the organization of available knowledge be? The possibilities range from information professionals to end users, from individual employees to departments and mixed project teams.

End users certainly have the best understanding of the work context in which the knowledge in question is going to be used. However, they generally do not know how to best develop appropriate structures.

This is where professionals with a background in library and information science come in. They are experts in organizing knowledge. The challenge for them lies in understanding the users' requirements, the subject matter of the knowledge to be organized, and the overall strategic goals of the company in sufficient detail.

If developing a knowledge structure just means creating twenty folders for a small group of people who interact on a daily basis, or drawing a simple knowledge map in order to remind such a group where they can get important knowledge from, then employing experts for this purpose will of course be overkill.

Developing knowledge structures

If, on the other hand, organizing knowledge constitutes a major effort, such as creating or adapting a large classification scheme, experience suggests that it is usually not a good idea to leave that task to either end users or information technology departments. The reason is simple: Although a challenge, it is generally easier for information professionals to understand the users' perspective than it would be for users or technology experts to digest all the necessary background knowledge about the different possibilities for organizing knowledge.

Information professionals will consider the needs of different types of users, for example production line workers and top management, the sales department and the research department, and employees and customers. End users will, of course, be involved.

Experience shows that what users want, and what they think they need, is not necessarily the same as what they actually need in order to get their jobs done effectively and efficiently. Therefore, users are often asked to participate in structure building techniques such as card sorting, where they arrange topics according to their own mental models rather than having to explain those models.

Since any large scale organization of knowledge will be quite expensive, such a project should either be recognized as being of strategic importance, and accordingly be staffed with information professionals, or else be abandoned altogether rather than conducted half-heartedly. After all, the costs incurred by introducing an unsuitable way of organizing knowledge are not just the costs of conducting the project itself. Much more importantly, they also include all the costs associated with the productivity lost by employees using that unsuitable solution in their daily work.

Assigning content to structures
So far, the question was who should be involved in determining which structure to use. The next step is to actually fill that structures with content. Whose job should it be to associate, for example, a given set of documents with suitable categories?

Information professionals are skilled in handling very large and complex structures, which end users cannot be expected to understand in sufficient detail. With small to medium sized structures, however, end users may be able to classify items even according to schemes which they could never have built by themselves. After all, this task only requires an understanding of the structure used, and not of all the reasons why that structure took its present form. Having all employees concerned perform this assignment themselves of course yields particularly good results when the content in question has not been acquired form external sources, but has been created by those employees themselves.

In some cases, it even makes sense to not only let end users take control of a controlled vocabulary, but to also do it at the point of retrieval rather then statically associating documents with elements of a structure.

For example, synonyms are usually either provided in advance by indexers or, in the case of full-text searching, they are specified by the user. Here, it is possible to provide control over synonyms through an additional layer containing search strategies (developed either by information professionals or based on previous searches) at the interface level [105].

Chapter 8

Transferring Knowledge

All the knowledge collected by a company will only amount to a huge, useless knowledge junkyard unless it is transferred to those people who actually create value by putting that knowledge to use. This chapter looks at different ways to transfer knowledge, provides some guidance on how to choose an appropriate method, considers the role of filtering and the presentation of knowledge, and finally takes a look at the transfer of tacit knowledge.

Knowledge Pull

If a transfer of knowledge is initiated by the knowledge seeker, this is called knowledge pull. If, on the other hand, knowledge is being delivered without the receiver having to become active, this is referred to as knowledge push.

Pull vs. push

In face-to-face settings, knowledge pull may happen either in a planned way, such as visiting a colleague in her office down the hall, or in an ad-hoc fashion, for instance after meeting a colleague at the water cooler.

Even some forms of knowledge transfer which are primarily associated with knowledge push, for example a lecture given by an expert, may sometimes derive most of their value from the knowledge pull that happens in the question period after the lecture. The same applies to institutionalized forms of knowledge transfer such as tutoring and mentoring.

In large organizations, knowledge transfer between different departments tends to be particularly difficult to achieve. The reasons for this are usually related to the dominant orga-

Knowledge fairs

nizational culture rather than any technical issues. One way to tackle this problem is to hold knowledge fairs.

The idea here is to encourage knowledge transfer across departmental boundaries by providing an environment that is as informal as possible while still offering some basic structure through the individual stands, which are usually organized by subject area or by project.

Of course conversations between people are not only important as a way of directly transferring knowledge, but also as a way of locating experts on a certain subject. This is where the real value of informal networks becomes apparent: By leveraging not only direct connections (asking colleagues what they know), but also indirect ones (asking colleagues who else might know something), the number of potential knowledge sources increases dramatically. In addition, the pointers to experts one receives from colleagues usually come with background information on those experts, thus permitting an informed choice.

Enabling knowledge transfer by providing pointers to experts can significantly benefit from information technology support. Solutions addressing this issue range from simple yellow pages applications with manually maintained employee profiles to sophisticated systems using expertise profiling, which analyze sources like documents authored by employees and email traffic in order to construct constantly updated guesses as to who might be an expert in which domain.

This is a direct answer to one of the lessons learned in chapter 3: Technology should connect people with each other. Two other lessons learned must not be forgotten in this context either. First, users must always be in control of how the system deals with data about them, otherwise they will not be able to correct the occasional wrong guess of the system, which will then quickly acquire a very bad reputation among employees. Second, privacy issues must be resolved in a way that ensures both the peace of mind of the employees and the overall usefulness of the system.

Pulling knowledge directly from electronic sources is usually referred to as knowledge retrieval. It would be rather pointless to descend into philosophical discussions about the nature of knowledge retrieval versus information retrieval here. Knowledge retrieval is probably best conceived as an integrated, value-added solution incorporating many of the techniques from classical information retrieval. Accordingly, many of the associated issues are very similar. There are two basic approaches: Searching and browsing.

Users often prefer typing some keywords and hoping for the best rather than systematically following links until they find what they need. The trouble with this approach is that users are rarely good at constructing effective search queries. In fact, most users will provide only one or two keywords and not use any logical operators at all [81, 176].

Searching

The problem is exacerbated by the fact that not all search engines use the same query syntax. While there is still room for improvement of the technologies handling such imprecise queries, guessing what the user really means is only possible up to a certain point, even for the best technology. Ultimately, it is therefore the human element which needs to be addressed here. This again emphasizes the lesson learned about the need to develop knowledge skills.

Browsing often yields better results for the knowledge seeker, but it also requires more effort on the part of the knowledge provider. In order to make it possible for users to browse effectively, the system needs a certain amount of structural information about all the objects in a repository.

Browsing

Text documents, for instance, would ideally not only contain more links (both within the document and to other documents) than typical documents do today, but also be classified according to a widely accepted, publicly available classification scheme as well as one particular to the company, and would contain lots of metadata as well as usage histories. Similarly, other types of objects in a repository, for instance items representing persons or projects, will not aid browsing unless there is abundant interlinking.

While some documented knowledge may reside locally on a employee's personal computer, most of it will usually be fetched from some other server on the network. This raises the issue of how to best transfer items of knowledge between various systems. They can either be transferred in an internal knowledge representation format, leaving the job of rendering them into a piece of text or graphics to the client machine, or the rendering can already happen on the server, leaving only the display of the preprocessed content to the client.

In practice, the choice will depend on both the application in question and on the existing information technology infrastructure. Rendering content on servers will require more powerful servers, but reduce the demands on the client, which is particularly important for mobile applications accessed through networked personal digital assistants or smartphones.

Knowledge Push

Methods for the delivery of knowledge that are not initiated by the receiver, but rather by some other person or system, are collectively referred to as knowledge push. This does not necessarily mean that the delivery will take the receiver by surprise. In fact, it is often the receiver himself who sets up the delivery criteria in advance, for instance by telling a system to alert him to any new documents published under a certain category. The choice may also be made by someone else, however, as in the case of an internal newsletter distributed to all employees.

 Knowledge push from one person to another occurs both in an ad-hoc fashion, for example in a conversation following a chance encounter of employees on the corridor, or as an institutionalized activity, for instance in the form of periodic meetings in which all members of a department are kept up to date about what is happening in various projects. Internal training courses may also be regarded as a form of knowledge push.

 Information technology supports knowledge push in two ways. Generic communication technologies such as email and instant messaging often form the basis of knowledge push both from one person to another and from systems to people. Similarly, portals are not per se knowledge push technologies, but usually include some push features, such as a window displaying important company news on the start page.

On the other hand, there are technologies specifically developed for knowledge push. Many digital libraries, for example, feature a service to alert users to new issues of their preferred periodicals. Often, they also allow users to specify arbitrary searches which will be conducted regularly by the system. Users will then automatically be alerted to any new results from their customized searches.

Knowledge push may not only be initiated by events, as in the example of the new document alert, or time, as in the example of the newsletter, but also be based on user behavior. Someone writing a project proposal in a word processor, for example, might be alerted to the existence of relevant background information in a corporate repository. Another example would be a system showing documents associated with the person the user is currently communicating with.

Relevance based on context

While people are generally very good at understanding the work context of their peers and offering helpful advice tailored to their current situation, systems observing the user's behavior and then drawing the user's attention to knowledge relevant to his current actions are still in their infancy.

In order to provide that kind of assistance, a system needs information about the user's actions, the content the user is working on, and the usage history of the repository. Getting at the content may be easy when dealing with word processors, but becomes a challenge with telephone conversations. Access to the usage history of the repository is necessary for the system to avoid suggesting documents the user already knows.

Furthermore, the challenge here lies not just in interpreting the user's actions and inferring what knowledge might be useful, but also in estimating the reliability of those inferences: How confident is the system in its estimate of the relevance of a particular knowledge item? Is it justified to actually interrupt the users work?

Those kinds of decisions will also have to take the disruptiveness of the user interface into account: Are the system's suggestions being shown in a centered popup window, in a small window at the corner of the screen, or is there just a tiny icon somewhere?

Choosing a Method

Obviously, a wide variety of methods for knowledge transfer is available. But how to choose one for a particular task? First, it is important to realize that this decision cannot always be made in advance, in the planning stage of a project. Instead, the decision will often have to be made on the spot when the particular requirements become clear. A lesson learned is pertinent here: Offer multiple channels for knowledge transfer.

Offer several methods

This is not to say that all methods have to be offered at all times. Knowledge planning and, perhaps even more importantly, a pilot project will show which selection of methods sensibly should be offered to knowledge workers in a particular context.

Amount and kind of knowledge

In order to choose an appropriate method of knowledge transfer, both the amount and the kind of knowledge to be transferred have to be taken into account. For example, if the task is to transfer knowledge about some abstract mathematical discovery, one would choose whichever method of transfer best supports explanations, because the primary concern here is to make it as easy as possible for the receiver to understand that discovery.

The transfer of tacit knowledge, on the other hand, will often require a completely different approach. In the martial arts, for instance, observation, imitation, and learning by doing are generally much more important than explicit explanations.

Source and receiver

Communication skills

Both the source and the receiver of knowledge have to be considered as well. People may be willing to provide knowledge, but be unavailable for face-to-face conversations because of their location. They may also be on a tight schedule. Their communication skills, or lack thereof, might also rule out some types of transfer. Finally, the role of personal relationships between the source and the receiver should not be underestimated.

If, on the other hand, the source is a computer system, factors influencing the decision will include the degree of formalization of the knowledge contained in the system, the user interface, and whether the system is capable of intelligently reacting to user behavior.

The receiver may be limited by time constraints, too. Prior knowledge will also play a crucial role, as will individual learning styles: Some people focus on interpersonal communication, some find it easier to absorb knowledge through written stories, while others benefit more from abstractions, visual images, or even musical or kinesthetic methods [166].

If the receiver is a computer system, the obvious question is whether it will able to handle all aspects of the knowledge being offered or only absorb some of it. This will depend on both the transfer mechanism and the format used to represent knowledge within the system.

Ultimately, the appropriateness of a method of knowledge transfer is not only determined by its effectiveness, but also by its efficiency. The knowledge to be transferred has to arrive at its destination, but in a business context, it also has to do so at reasonable cost.

Effectiveness and efficiency

In assessing costs associated with knowledge transfer, attention has to be paid on the one hand to implementation, including both organizational and information technology expenses, and on the other hand to running costs incurred by usage. Looking at those costs is, of course, only meaningful in relation to the benefits brought by knowledge transfer, and it is estimating those benefits that usually constitutes the hard part.

Dixon [47] offers a typology of knowledge transfer processes, design guidelines for each type, and advice on how to choose an appropriate method. She distinguishes between Serial Transfer, Near Transfer, Far Transfer, Strategic Transfer, and Expert Transfer.

Five types of knowledge transfer

In Serial Transfer, both tacit and explicit knowledge is transferred within a team performing similar, frequent but nonroutine tasks in different settings, for instance replacing power generators at different sites. Design guidelines for Serial Transfer include regular but brief, locally facilitated meetings in which everyone involved participates, and avoiding recriminations.

Near Transfer is characterized by the transfer of explicit knowledge about similar, frequent, and routine tasks between teams working in a similar context, for example sharing process improvements between manufacturing plants. Design guidelines for Near Transfer include electronic knowledge push of a limited number of items taken from a targeted database containing brief descriptions. This should be supplemented by personal interaction, and usage as well as business goals should be monitored.

Far Transfer deals with transferring tacit knowledge about similar, frequent but nonroutine tasks between teams working in different contexts, for example through peers assisting colleagues at an oil exploration site and discovering new approaches through that collaboration. Design guidelines for Far Transfer include carrying knowledge across the organization by people, reciprocal exchange, and a recognizable name for the initiative.

Strategic Transfer refers to the transfer of both explicit and tacit knowledge about infrequent and nonroutine tasks between teams operating in different contexts affecting the whole organization. An example for this would be a company acquiring another company, and some months later reusing the lessons learned in that process when another team handles the acquisition of a further company. Design guidelines for Strategic Transfer include senior-level managers identifying relevant knowledge, specialists collecting knowledge in real time rather than retrospectively, and synthesizing multiple voices.

Finally, Expert Transfer is concerned with transferring explicit knowledge about different, infrequent but routine tasks performed by different teams in a similar context, such as technicians asking for and getting advice on out-of-date equipment from an email list. Design guidelines for Expert Transfer include knowledge pull from supported electronic forums that are segmented by topic, and encouragement of differing levels of participation.

As a simplified way of choosing a type of transfer, Dixon suggests looking at who will be using the knowledge to be transferred, whether the knowledge is explicit or tacit, whether the task is routine and frequent, and whether the whole organization is concerned. If lessons learned by a team are going to be reused by that same team, Serial Transfer is called for. Otherwise, if only explicit knowledge is to be transferred, the decision is between Expert Transfer and Near Transfer, the latter being used in case of a routine and frequent task. If, on the other hand, tacit knowledge needs to be transferred, Strategic Transfer covers cases in which the knowledge has an impact on the whole organization, otherwise the case is one for Far Transfer.

Filtering Knowledge

Transfer only appropriate knowledge

The aim of transferring knowledge is not to transfer just any knowledge that happens to be available. Rather, knowledge available from whatever source—people, paper, or electronic content—needs to be filtered in order to ensure that only knowledge which is actually useful to the receiver is being transferred.

In judging the usefulness of knowledge to the receiver, two sets of criteria have to be taken into account. First, there are the general characteristics of the receiver, such as educational background and function in the company. Second, the situation in which the transfer of knowledge occurs needs to be considered. This may, for example, be the context of a particular project the receiver is working on.

The filtering process is influenced by a number of factors [58]. First among these is the authority and credibility of the source of information. Authority may be based on the generally acknowledged competence of a source, for instance in the case of a world-renowned expert on a particular subject, or it may derive from the position or role of an individual in the company. There may also be an intermediate instance that adds the seal of authority to items of knowledge through a review process.

Factors
influencing
filtering

Another factor consists of the biases of the receiver, which make objective judgment almost impossible. This is a vicious circle: Filtering through those biases reinforces the beliefs of the receiver, which in turn makes objective judgment even harder the next time. The personal experiences of the receiver influence the filtering process in a similar way. It is particularly important to realize this in connection with incentive schemes in knowledge management.

The intellectual skills the receiver needs in order to assess given items of knowledge constitute a further factor influencing the filtering process. Finally, there is the desperation factor: Having searched in vain for a long time, many people desperately looking for an answer to a particular question will accept almost any information they eventually find. This something-beats-nothing attitude of course undermines any attempt at objectively assessing the information in question.

What does all this mean in practice? First, the need to consider the receiver's general characteristics and current situation implies that for someone looking for knowledge, it may often make more sense to talk to a reasonably competent colleague at work than consulting a brilliant expert who does not know anything about the particular situation.

Practical
consequences

For the same reason, people whose job is to review knowledge from a variety of different sources will add much more value if they personally know the employees concerned and are familiar with their work. This way, they can actually judge the relevance of knowledge, not just the authority of its source. The problems of overcoming receivers' biases, building up the necessary intellectual skills, and not falling prey to the desperation factor once again underline a lesson learned: Do not underestimate the need to develop knowledge skills.

While filtering based on current context is the ideal to strive for, context-independent filter criteria sometimes also have their place. In a company subscribing to a number of different electronic newsfeeds, for instance, a department may choose to filter out all items from certain sources deemed irrelevant for that department's needs.

Balance between filtering and capturing

Finally, it is important to realize that there is a trade-off between filtering knowledge and not capturing irrelevant knowledge in the first place. Capturing almost everything just in case it might turn out to be useful at some point is not only very expensive, but also makes filtering more difficult: A more sophisticated approach to filtering will be required to deal with the huge amount and varied nature of all the knowledge collected.

On the other hand, deciding precisely which knowledge should be captured is also very difficult. It will often be next to impossible to judge whether a given piece of knowledge might be useful sometime in the future. A balance between what to capture and what to filter has to be found based on the specific requirements and experiences of the company in question.

Presenting Knowledge

Intelligibility of knowledge

Imagine that you are being offered just the knowledge you need (in other words, appropriately filtered), and just in time (thanks to the right choice of transfer medium)—but when you look at it, all you see is a long string of zeroes and ones. Obviously, the form of presentation also plays a major role in successful knowledge transfer.

Communication skills

As with choosing a medium and with filtering, the challenge again lies in adapting to the receiver and his current context. In face-to-face knowledge transfer, this means that the people sharing their knowledge should not only be competent in the subject area, but also possess good communication skills. Unlike professional communicators, the best experts in a field are often focused very tightly on their work. It might never occur to them to attend a course to improve their communication skills.

In addition, knowledge push is not always easily accepted, even if everyone involved is aware of its necessity. This may be due to simple reasons like time constraints, or to the nature of the knowledge in question. Breaking bad news to a colleague at an inopportune time in a productive way, for example, will require much better communication skills than telling people that their proposal has been accepted. It is up to management to remove those barriers to knowledge transfer. First, awareness has to be raised. Then, opportunities have to be created for employees to improve their communication skills.

Narratives are a particularly interesting form of packaging knowledge. The main reason why purposeful storytelling is such a powerful way of presenting knowledge is because stories focusing on persons and actions make it easy for the listener to grasp the meaning of what is being said. Good stories are tailored to the target audience: The knowledge to be transferred is wrapped in a story about what is important to the listener.

Storytelling

If the people involved in the transfer of knowledge come from different backgrounds, bridging that gap will be critical. Ideally, the persons sharing their knowledge will be familiar with each others' domains of expertise. In practice, however, flexible minds and experience with this kind of situation—not necessarily with the same domains—may ultimately prove to be almost as useful.

Subject expertise

For transferring knowledge with the help of information technology rather than face-to-face, the choice of an appropriate medium is crucial. Mobile phones and desktop computers, for instance, have very different advantages and drawbacks.

The task of presentation now is to embed items of knowledge in as much context as possible without overwhelming the user. When retrieving documents from a repository, this can mean showing where they fit into a classification scheme and displaying document summaries, annotations, and links to related documents as well as other objects representing people or projects.

Displaying content

Since documents often contain a wealth of material, summaries will ideally be created dynamically in order to focus on the relationship of the document to current interests of the user. This can be accomplished for example by taking recent search queries into account and attaching more weight to the terms contained in those queries.

All of the possibilities mentioned can either be shown in an overview of several different documents, for instance in the case of search results, or they can be incorporated into the documents themselves. The presentation of the documents themselves may also be created dynamically for each user, taking account of that user's particular needs (for example whether or not to display a summary) and preferences (for instance regarding the font size) [74].

Paying attention to details like font size is important for two reasons. First, their impact on how quickly and easily the material is assimilated by the reader is often underestimated. Second, the acceptance of the system on the part of the users may depend upon such details to a significant extent.

Visualization   Visualization techniques ranging from innovative ways of viewing hierarchical structures like classification schemes to elaborate three-dimensional virtual worlds are increasingly being employed in knowledge management applications. The human brain is capable of taking in and analyzing visual features like patterns and colors at an astonishing rate. Through appropriate visualization techniques, this fact can be used to reduce the cognitive load on the user: The context of items of knowledge is presented in a way that can be understood quickly and easily instead of requiring tedious reading and interpreting of text.

Portals   Finally, portals draw relevant knowledge from disparate sources and present it in a coherent and contextualized way. While most information technology tools supporting knowledge presentation do so primarily by dealing with the context of knowledge within the system, the main focus of portals typically is on the work context of the user, for instance by offering a specific environment for marketing and another one for product development.

Transferring Tacit Knowledge

The transfer of tacit knowledge is a particular challenge since it is usually not only harder to accomplish than the transfer of explicit knowledge, but usually also takes much more time. A typical example for this are apprenticeships in the crafts.

The point here is that tacit knowledge generally cannot be taught. It can only be picked up over time. Job rotation often helps to transfer tacit knowledge within organizations. Communities of practice can provide opportunities for transferring tacit knowledge, too. To a certain extent, coaching may also help.

Among the various kinds of communication between people, narratives stand the best chance of getting across tacit knowledge. Unlike abstract reasoning, storytelling appeals to emotions and conveys elements of tacit knowledge like attitudes in a way people can grasp intuitively.

Technology is often regarded as being of little help when it comes to transferring tacit knowledge. Discounting the role of technology may be premature, however. Consider electronic forums on the intranets of large companies as an example. By browsing through past discussions, new employees not only become acquainted with the issues discussed, but also get a feeling for prevailing opinions, attitudes, and organizational culture in general.

The role of technology in transferring tacit knowledge can be analyzed by drawing on a distinction between data, information, and knowledge [16]. As an example of explicit knowledge transfer, consider a supplier receiving a production forecast (explicit knowledge) through intermediate steps involving order forms (data) and a production schedule (information) from clients' sales forecasts (explicit knowledge). As an example of tacit knowledge transfer, take designers transferring knowledge by expressing their design skills (tacit knowledge) through drafts (information) and graphic files (data).

As far as technology support is concerned, the difference between explicit and tacit knowledge transfer can now be attributed to the levels supported in each case: In the case of explicit knowledge transfer, technology can directly support the handling of both data and information. In the case of tacit knowledge transfer, by contrast, technology support only makes sense at the data level. The transfer of tacit knowledge still appears as a more challenging task than the transfer of explicit knowledge, but the role of technology is acknowledged in both cases.

Chapter 9

Maintaining Knowledge

One of the important lessons learned in chapter 3 has been that there is a need for ongoing maintenance of knowledge. This chapter discusses that process in more detail. First, the requirements for knowledge maintenance are clarified by considering the various business drivers which make this process necessary in the first place. After that, the different kinds of knowledge that have to be maintained are identified. A description of actions to be taken in order to maintain that knowledge follows. Finally, the question of who should be responsible for maintaining knowledge is considered.

The Importance of Maintaining Knowledge

In order to have any positive effect, knowledge must meet several criteria. First of all, of course, it has to be available. Companies usually find it hard to benefit from knowledge in the heads of employees who suddenly become ex-employees. But knowledge also has to be accurate and up to date. Misinformation or misinterpretations must not be allowed to become part of the organizational knowledge base.

Available, accurate, and up to date knowledge

A number of factors faced by companies today threaten to erode the knowledge that is available, accurate, and up to date. The downsizing wave has led companies to part with many employees—and with their knowledge. The contribution of middle management, in particular, was often underestimated.

Downsizing

Exacerbating the problem, today's dynamic labor market for knowledge workers means that employees change jobs frequently, again taking their knowledge with them. Out-

Resignations, outsourcing

sourcing can also contribute to the problem if the focus is exclusively on short-term cost savings and no attention is paid to the consequences for the availability of key knowledge.

The problem with losing key employees is not just one of keeping knowledge available, but also of keeping it up to date. Suppose, for example, that an expert who recently left the company had documented all of her knowledge, and that is now available in a corporate repository. This is, of course, in itself impossible, but even in that "ideal" case, all the company would be left with is a snapshot of that expert's knowledge at a particular point in time. Very soon, much of that knowledge will be out of date, while the expert herself will continuously keep her own knowledge up to date. Had the company retained her as an employee, it would have ensured its access to that up to date knowledge.

Security concerns

Failing to pay attention to security concerns can also lead to the loss of key knowledge. This might happen through accidents, for example if an employee mistakenly deletes valuable records and no backup has been made, or it might even happen through deliberate attacks, for instance by hackers breaking into a company's network.

Changes in the environment

Changes in the business environment constantly undermine the validity of any static collection of knowledge. Missing major changes in the markets might well spell the untimely demise of a company. However, even knowledge about minor changes, for instance a change of the contact person in a partner company, must not be missed and may in fact be crucial for projecting a professional image.

Changes in content

Finally, changes made to various kinds of content, be it in electronic form or on paper, may make some related knowledge inaccurate. On the technical side, this can simply mean avoiding link inconsistencies. Relevant knowledge residing in people's heads also needs to be maintained: A key account manager, for instance, has to be aware of the current version as well as the version history of documents he is referring to when talking to a client.

Kinds of Knowledge to Maintain

Which kinds of knowledge need to be maintained? Three broad classes can be distinguished. In the case of documented knowledge, both the content itself and the structure in which it is embedded will have to be dealt with. When it comes to knowledge in people's heads, employees and networks of people take center stage.

When maintaining content, the most important issue is that of quality versus quantity. Ensuring either of the two will require substantial effort, and going for both is usually neither affordable nor sensible. Opting for quality rather than indiscriminate quantity will make more sense for most organizations. The big consultancies, for example, naturally produce a lot of documented knowledge. But rather than swamping their databases and drowning their employees with all of that, they invest heavily in selecting and aggregating high-quality content for reuse. **Content**

Maintaining content also means paying attention to language. The use of language changes over time: New terms may appear but denote the same concept as old ones, and old terms may undergo a change of meaning. This highlights the role controlled vocabularies can play.

A controlled vocabulary may simply be a list of terms that are supposed to be used consistently across the organization, for instance to avoid the frequent case of marketing and engineering departments talking about the same thing, but using different words for it and failing to understand each other as a result. Controlled vocabularies can, however, be much more than simple lists of terms: They can include information about different relationships between terms. In other words, controlled vocabularies can be structured.

Maintaining structures used for organizing knowledge can be a particular challenge. In the case of a simple controlled vocabulary, this structure will often be easily manageable. The classification schemes used for large document repositories, however, tend to be huge. Their maintenance usually requires specialists, typically with a background in library and information science. **Structure**

Things get even more demanding if the structure in question is not restricted to a simple hierarchy, but may contain loops and different types of relationships. Even with all the experience gained in the field of knowledge engineering over the past decades, maintaining complex ontologies still remains a challenge.

In addition to those kinds of structure, which are external to any given document, there is also the structure inherent in many documents to consider. Not every bit of text is born equal: Some represent just plain body text, but others are headings, references, and links to other documents.

Making this kind of structure explicit is the idea behind markup languages like HTML, the language in which most web pages are written. However, this only solves the problem of easily parsing documents and extracting their internal structure. These structural elements still have to be maintained, as in the case of links to documents which may not exist any more.

People   The most valuable knowledge, however, usually resides only in the heads of employees. Maintaining that knowledge effectively requires an approach firmly connecting knowledge management considerations with human resources practices. Skills management is called for.

In the long run, it is important to maintain not only knowledge that is available now, but also sources of future knowledge. Databases which are not currently being used, but which may, together with others, be useful for future data mining activities, are a case in point.

Most important in that context, however, is the maintenance of networks of people, both within the organization and beyond. Communities of practice spanning company boundaries can be particularly valuable sources of knowledge, but like all social relationships they will simply fade away and die if neglected for too long.

Knowledge Maintenance Tasks

Having gained an impression of the importance of maintaining knowledge and of the different kinds of knowledge that need to be maintained, the question now is: What are the actual tasks that have to be performed under the umbrella of maintaining knowledge? Five basic ones can be distinguished: Reviewing, correcting and updating, refining, preserving, and removing.

Reviewing   The first step naturally is to review the knowledge in question. Some kinds of knowledge, for instance about current events, require constant attention, while others should be subjected to periodic review but do not really need to be maintained constantly.

For key knowledge that has been identified as absolutely critical to the organization's success, it may be warranted to have that knowledge independently validated either in-house or, if its quality is in doubt but it is not confidential, also by outside experts. This is the quality assurance part. Addressing quantity, the review process should also help determine knowledge gaps. This is closely linked to the more general process of assessing knowledge, which is discussed in chapter 10.

Reviewing the structure of a repository should include both making sure that documents have been assigned to the correct categories, and that the categories themselves still make sense in the light of recent business developments. As so often, people and technology-based approaches are complementary here. Automatic classification, for instance, may save a lot of work, but its results may have to be checked by subject experts.

Reviewing the state of employees' knowledge and of networks of people is a particular challenge since it requires the involvement of many people. However, the results may well be worth the effort. Diagrams visualizing relationships between people, in particular, often help not only to identify hubs of knowledge hitherto unrecognized as such, but can also be used to track the development of networks over time, paving the way for targeted support measures.

Approaches aiming more directly at making the knowledge held by employees visible for the purposes of maintaining that knowledge will ideally also be integrated with steps taken to build yellow pages or similar systems. Again, there are connections to the more general kinds of knowledge assessment described in chapter 10.

If the review reveals any errors, then of course the next step will be to correct those. Errors may either be factual errors, where the presumed knowledge has been inaccurate or simply false from the beginning, or they may have crept in over time as the knowledge in question became outdated.

Correcting and updating

Whatever the cause, correcting or updating knowledge can take a number of forms. Apart from changes to the content itself, for instance the text of a document, updating can also mean restructuring. A conference description, for example, would be moved from the "Current events" folder to the "Past events" folder, and links might be added to the conference proceedings or to reports by attendees.

If documents are updated, it is usually a good idea to keep the original version available, as many people may have referenced it. But a note that this constitutes outdated material and add a link to the updated version should be added. Much of this can be automated.

Bringing structures up to date usually requires human judgment, but can often be supported by technology. For example, clustering technologies applied to recently added content of a repository may give an indication about which of the categories currently in use need to be updated.

Staff training certainly qualifies as a kind of knowledge maintenance as well; after all, it serves to update the knowledge of employees. Together with other forms of providing up to date knowledge to employees, for instance through coaching, it is best managed through a systematic skills management approach.

For networks of people, updating can be interpreted not only in the sense of keeping track of peoples' contact addresses and changes in their interests, but also in the sense of deliberately shifting one's attention to certain relationships because of changes in one's own interests.

Refining   Apart from discovering that it is necessary to correct or

update knowledge, the review may also suggest that it would be good idea to refine some of that knowledge: To add more detail, or to represent documented knowledge in form more suited either to be interpreted by people or to be processed by systems. This applies to both content and structures.

Refining employees' knowledge, like updating it, is addressed by skills management. Refining networks of people means deliberately taking measures to extend them. The mechanisms typically employed for refining knowledge are the same as those for integrating and organizing knowledge, which are discussed in chapters 6 and 7.

Preserving   Beyond providing knowledge for immediate use, it should also be preserved for the long term. Regarding people, this implies going to great lengths in order to retain key employees.

Recognizing that this cannot not always be successful, the approach sounding most promising to many managers is to have employees document as much of their knowledge as possible before they leave the company. This is discussed as one form of integrating knowledge in chapter 6, and it turns out to be one of the toughest challenges in knowledge management. Generally, therefore, fostering a certain degree of redundancy of employees' knowledge through overlaps between their areas of expertise seems highly advisable.

A simple but effective way to help preserve employees' knowledge for use by the organization is to keep track of their career history. The idea is to make sure that not only the current job is known about an employee, but also previous positions both within the company and elsewhere.

If employees do leave, which of course they invariably will, knowledge-focused exit interviews may preserve some of their knowledge for the organization. The same basic idea can be implemented with regard to employees heading for retirement. In that case, it will be a planned activity over a longer period of time rather than a last minute resort, and correspondingly more effective.

As already pointed out in chapter 6, maintaining ties with former employees after they have left, for instance through alumni networks, may also contribute to preserving knowledge.

Preserving the content and structure of documented knowledge essentially boils down to two tasks. The first is to store them in a way that protects them against anything that might lead to their loss. The second is to keep them not only accessible, but actually interpretable.

Regarding storage, regular backups and archiving serve to limit the danger posed by various security risks ranging from accidents to deliberate attacks by outsiders or even frustrated employees seeking revenge. The choice of suitable media and a safe physical location play an important role here. In this context, the backup computing centers maintained by many large companies can be regarded not only as a safeguard against disrupting operations, but also as a storehouse preserving documented knowledge.

Just being able to access some files containing critical knowledge is not enough, however. One also has to be able to process those files, to interpret their content. With the rapid succession of new versions of software packages today, many of them introducing new proprietary file formats, this cannot be taken for granted. If a company switches from one software package to another, the new one might not be able to read older files. Indeed, even newer versions of some software packages by leading vendors today sometimes cannot read their own predecessors' files. Adhering to established standards offers a way out. Chapter 20 provides an overview of relevant standards.

Hardware issues also have to be considered: Backup tapes are useless without appropriate tape drives. Generations of hardware devices typically follow each other less quickly than software versions, but taking the long-term view, one will have to take them into account as well in order to preserve knowledge.

Removing Finally, the verdict of reviewing knowledge can also be that some of the knowledge in question should be treated as a liability rather than as an asset, that it constitutes unnecessary baggage, incurring costs through storage and administration and, more importantly, distracting the attention of employees, without contributing to organizational goals. Such knowledge has to be removed from organizational memory.

Documented knowledge stored in a repository can simply be deleted. The situation is more complicated with knowledge residing in employees' heads. Strategies for deliberate organizational forgetting will always be highly dependent on the dominant culture in that organization. For networks of people, by contrast, the solution is technically simple, albeit not particularly nice: "High maintenance" contacts that are judged to be surplus can simply be broken off.

Note that there is also a legal dimension to the decision of whether to preserve or remove content. Some records must not be destroyed. On the other hand, there are also cases in which keeping archives is not mandated by anyone, but which can have legal consequences. Emails, for instance, have been admitted as evidence in courts. Depending on the situation, they may either serve as a defense or incriminate a company—one's own, a business partner, or a competitor.

The substantial effort spent on setting up a comprehensive and consistent structure for a knowledge repository usually means that one will hardly be tempted to carelessly throw it away as superfluous. In some cases, however, proper knowledge maintenance may really require switching to a different structure and discarding the old one.

Even in such cases, however, salvaging previous work may be possible to some extent, for instance by mapping one classification scheme onto another and thereby rescuing most of the effort that went into classifying knowledge according to the original scheme.

Simpler structural elements, such hyperlinks between documents, generally only need to be removed if the target document becomes unavailable for some reason. Usually link management components of content management systems automatically take care of this.

Responsibilities for Maintaining Knowledge

What remains to be discussed is who in the organization should be responsible for maintaining knowledge. Keeping fundamental knowledge of employees up to date and refining it through training, as well as preserving knowledge by retaining employees, is usually the task of management and the human resources department.

Management and human resources

The answer is less clear for maintaining the content and structure of knowledge repositories. Such repositories will of course often be intranet applications, but one should not forget about the role of traditional libraries either.

Librarians

This already points to one possible answer: Corporate librarians are familiar not only with the theory and practice of maintaining documented knowledge in many forms, but also with the company and its knowledge requirements. Even if they might have to learn some aspects of a new technology, this can usually be accomplished much more quickly than having technology experts study library and information science. Employing a librarian to maintain the content and structure of a repository also takes the workload off the front-line employees.

On the other hand, while librarians typically have a better understanding of the big picture of knowledge sources and needs, they may sometimes be lacking accurate first-hand understanding of the details [64]. Companies where this is the rule rather than the exception are probably better off having all employees maintain whatever content they contributed. In order for this to work, it is crucial for management to point out the importance placed on maintaining knowledge and to give employees the time they need to actually do so.

Front-line employees

Finally, keeping in mind the lesson learned about the importance of establishing knowledge management roles, maintaining knowledge may also be the responsibility of specially created roles, which may be part-time, for instance something all project managers have to do, or a full-time job. Some of the big consultancies have multiple levels of such roles, and

Specially created roles

former active consultants are employed to maintain knowledge in their areas of experience [8].

Chapter 10

Assessing Knowledge

Assessing knowledge can take a number of forms. This chapter first provides an overview of different approaches. The most important contribution is made measuring intellectual capital. The chapter then describes the steps typically involved in such an endeavor: Strategic modeling, generating and selecting indicators, implementation and measurement, and interpretation and feedback.

Approaches to Assessing Knowledge

Having recognized that knowledge is a resource of the utmost importance, companies are naturally interested in assessing the knowledge available to them. There are two different views on when to undertake such an assessment. Many people see a thorough assessment of a company's knowledge as a precondition for any meaningful knowledge planning. Others argue that one should not delay a knowledge management initiative by focusing on measurements too soon; the idea is to get the initiative off the ground as quickly as possible and to introduce measurements later. Once knowledge management is established in an organization, assessment can serve to determine the extent to which goals set in knowledge planning have been reached.

When to assess knowledge

Unfortunately, trying to measure knowledge is a notoriously difficult endeavor. Quickly judging the success of individual knowledge management projects, as opposed to long-term initiatives, constitutes a particular challenge. In some cases measures may be found that capture the partic-

Judging the success of projects

ular contribution of one project. It may even be possible to calculate a return on investment.

More often, however, the very nature of knowledge management means that an individual project's contribution will be next to impossible to disentangle from other factors. There is a very real danger here: If expectations concerning the quick assessment of individual projects are too high, a knowledge management initiative might not survive long enough for the organization to really reap its benefits. This again emphasizes one of the lessons learned in chapter 3: Management commitment is important.

Rating items of knowledge

A more modest agenda for assessing knowledge is to only look at easily accessible items of knowledge in more detail. Documents in a repository, for instance, can be rated with regard to their quality and usefulness for particular target groups or tasks. Dimensions of quality include accuracy, comprehensiveness, timeliness, and relevance. Ratings can be established explicitly by asking the user ("Did this document help you?"), or they may be determined implicitly by analyzing usage statistics.

Individually, ratings help with maintaining knowledge: Something should be done about items that are hardly ever used, or even worse, frequently accessed but judged inadequate. Taken together, ratings paint a picture of the overall quality and usefulness of the documented knowledge available within the organization. Monitoring the changes of ratings over time reveals the increase or decline of the importance of various types and topics of knowledge.

Measuring intellectual capital

The biggest promise of assessing knowledge, however, is to be found on the strategic level. The most suitable instrument here is the measurement of intellectual capital. This approach is more general in scope in the sense that it aims to cover not just knowledge as such, but also other intangibles like processes, organizational culture, and relationships with customers, suppliers, and partners.

Traditional methods of reporting and accounting generally fail to assess this intellectual capital. While a few nonfinancial metrics, like customer satisfaction and process cycle times, have been monitored for quite some time, attempts to systematically measure intellectual capital in its entirety have emerged only recently. There are no accepted standards as to which indicators to use or even which categories of indicators to consider. There is, however, some agreement on how to approach the identification of suitable indicators for a particular organization, namely by using a top-down, strategy-driven process.

Intellectual capital gets measured for a number of different purposes. The most widespread use is to help management align organizational practices with strategy, and to monitor the performance of those practices. On the operational level, the purpose can also be to get a better grip on existing data for day-to-day use.

Another purpose is external reporting: An intellectual capital report is published in order to increase transparency for stakeholders. Both the intellectual capital report and the process of creating it can also serve as means of communication. Company goals and values are communicated not only to external stakeholders, but also to staff, helping them set priorities if different goals are in conflict in day-to-day operations.

Finally, some companies undertake the measurement of intellectual capital with a view to benchmarking, although this tends to be a very elusive goal since indicators are hardly ever comparable between companies.

These purposes place somewhat different requirements on a framework for measuring intellectual capital. In particular, management will typically be more interested in short-term changes in the levels of intellectual capital rather than absolute numbers. Outside observers, on the other hand, will not be as familiar with the company and usually look at the measures less often. They want to get an idea of the current position of the company in relation to its competitors, and are therefore primarily interested in stocks of intellectual capital.

Can the measurement of intellectual capital be used as an out-of-the-box instrument to quickly evaluate the success or failure of knowledge management? No, not out-of-the-box (an adaptation of existing approaches is required for each particular organization), and not quickly (this adaptation and the implementation take considerable time and effort). In other words, if one is looking for some quick knowledge management metrics, this approach is not the way to go.

If, on the other hand, one is prepared to deal with the issue of intellectual capital on a strategic level, then through an appropriate choice of indicators this kind of approach may indeed not only provide new insights about the organization,

Purposes of measuring

No quick answers

Benefits of measuring

but also help to assess the impact of knowledge management in general and sometimes even of individual knowledge management projects.

Furthermore, by increasing transparency, measuring intellectual capital can be expected to lead to better allocation of resources. Last but not least, intellectual capital reporting can also serve as an instrument for communicating organizational values and commitment, thereby not only measuring, but also positively influencing knowledge management activities within the organization.

Few objective measures

It is important, however, not to expect the measurement of intellectual capital to provide the same level of objectiveness and comparability as traditional accounting. Since there is not nearly as much experience with interpreting intellectual capital indicators as there is with interpreting traditional financial ones, even comparing indicators over time within a single organization can be a challenge, and comparisons between different companies are often next to impossible.

Synergies with existing solutions

Assessing knowledge by measuring intellectual capital today usually takes the form of a strategic project not involving information technology staff. Potential synergies of that effort with knowledge management tools on the operational level are rarely realized. The content of yellow pages, results from automated expertise profiling, and usage patterns established by recommender systems could all be used as a basis for indicators that may be more meaningful than those typically used today.

Strategic Modeling

Coming up with a long list of indicators that are deemed to reflect a company's intellectual capital usually turns out to be surprisingly easy. But drowning in a sea of indicators is not the aim. The challenge is to settle on a small and manageable set of indicators. In order to determine which indicators are the most appropriate ones for a given company, the starting point should be that company's business strategy.

Business strategy as a starting point

Embarking on a project to measure intellectual capital without a clear idea of the business strategy will likely lead either to an instrument which is of little use or to the project being abandoned altogether. Should there be no consensus on strategic issues yet, it is essential that one is reached prior to proceeding with the attempt to measure intellectual capital. If constant redefinition of business goals, constant re-structuring, or a lack of open communication are typical for a company, then any initiative to measure intellectual capital will only have slim chances of success and the whole undertaking will probably not make much sense at all.

Strategic business goals should capture the essence of the business and the way it creates value, and for the purposes of measuring intellectual capital should be as specific to the company as possible. Based on a thorough understanding of strategic goals and the issues surrounding them, key success factors for reaching those goals can be identified. A cause and effect model can then be drawn up to show the relationships between strategic goals and key success factors as well as between the various factors. Care has to be taken to clearly document not only the end results of this step, but also the reasoning behind them.

From goals to success factors

In order to identify all relevant factors, it often helps to consider what different kinds of intellectual capital there are. One popular model distinguishes human capital and structural capital [136]. Human capital is subdivided into competence, attitude, and intellectual agility. Competence refers to the skills, experience, and education of employees. Attitude includes motivation, behavior (pertaining to the future success of the company), and conduct (pertaining to ethical values of society). Capacities for innovation, imitation, adaptation, and packaging make up the category intellectual agility.

Kinds of intellectual capital

Structural capital, on the other hand, is subdivided into relationships, organization, and renewal and development. The relationships category covers customers, suppliers, partners, shareholder, and other stakeholders. The organization category includes infrastructure, processes, and organizational culture. Finally, renewal and development is a catchall for everything else that is intangible and is expected to impact value in the future.

Of course things may also be considered from a financial perspective. However, it is argued that attempting to measure intellectual capital with the mindset and the tools of traditional accounting will obscure the perception of precisely those new aspects which provide the real value of an intellectual capital approach [157].

Deriving and prioritizing key success factors and indicators is also a great opportunity to make hitherto unnoticed trade-offs and conflicts of interest concerning the business at large become apparent. These activities often help to identify previously neglected cause and effect relationships as well. Lively discussion is the key to such insights. The process must not become a one-man-show.

Through discussions of why particular success factors are important enough to be pursued further, the mental models of the participants, in particular of top management, are explicated and a common language and a shared model are established. These can subsequently be communicated to others, for instance line management, in order to derive meaningful indicators.

Finally, an important effect of the discussions is also that the participants involved feel they own the process and accept the model created as a common result.

Generating and Selecting Indicators

The strategic model serves to guide the generation and selection of indicators capturing specifically those aspects of intellectual capital which are essential to the particular company. For each key success factor, a list of indicators reflecting that factor is drawn up through focused brainstorming sessions, personal interviews, or workshops involving line management and other experts on the operational processes concerned.

Indicators are observable variables and need to be defined precisely in order to avoid confusion later on. If the dimension of a proposed indicator (for instance cardinal, ordinal, currency units, or a dimensionless percentage) is unclear, a more accurate specification is called for. Typical examples for indicators are the percentage of employees holding an advanced degree, hours of training per employee per year, the average duration of employment in years, hours spent by senior staff to explain strategy and actions, and the number of suggestions made by employees per month [136].

A catalogue of indicators used by other companies may be helpful here, not through wholesale adoption, but as a way of stimulating ideas about what kinds of things can be measured in relation to the key success factors at hand.

In practice, even when focused on particular key success factors, long lists of possible indicators tend to be generated.

The challenge now is to select few but meaningful ones. Recommendations for the maximum total number of indicator range from about 10 to at most 50 [155, 157, 101].

It is important not to let political considerations guide indicator selection. The process of selecting indicators should be based on their usefulness and not degenerate either into a battlefield for turf wars or into an exercise in avoiding confrontation at all costs. A collection of "diplomatic" indicators that cannot harm anyone will be of interest to no one.

Three criteria have proven useful for selecting indicators. The validity of an indicator refers to how closely that indicator is related to the critical success factor in question. The other two criteria are concerned with the costs of measuring an indicator: An estimation of the one-time effort of establishing the means for data collection, and an estimation of the costs of ongoing data collection in subsequent measurement cycles.

Towards the end of the process of selecting indicators, it becomes necessary to test the balance of the list of indicators proposed as final. A good way to do this is to categorize the indicators using a model distinguishing different kinds of intellectual capital. If any of the categories of intellectual capital is represented by a conspicuously small or large number of indicators, this should be interpreted as a warning sign. In that case, unless the imbalance is warranted by the specific situation of the company, one will usually go over the selection again.

Ensuring balance

The hierarchical structure of intellectual capital outlined in the previous section is one categorization that can be used for checking the balance of the selection. Another, more comprehensive model takes the form of a table with six columns and three rows [4, 157]. Different kinds of intellectual capital make up the columns: Competence, internal structure, external structure, social citizenship, environmental health, and corporate identity. In addition, the rows of the table distinguish between indicators related to the growth and renewal, the efficiency, and the stability of the organization.

Since the different categorizations of intellectual capital all have their own strengths and weaknesses, it may make sense to use several different ones. It may also be useful to have a look at more specific categorizations which place a stronger emphasis on, for example, types of intellectual property.

Implementation and Measurement

All the activities related to measuring intellectual capital which have been discussed so far involve only an appointed project team as well as a handful of further participants in interviews and workshops. Once a set of indicators to use has been decided upon, however, the task becomes to collect the data necessary to actually express those indicators in numbers. This will often involve the organization at large, for instance through employee surveys.

Preparing for
data collection

In order to keep the effort required to a minimum, careful planning is essential. For each indicator, both the source and the time required to collect the necessary data should be clear in advance. Depending on the kind of indicators that have been chosen, it may be possible to automate data collection to a significant extent. For example, programming a simple script to extract the number of new records added to a bibliography database will save time in each subsequent measurement cycle.

As with any project involving data collection, special attention needs to be paid to the perspective of the contributors of data. Ideally, data collection will be embedded in existing work processes so as not to be perceived as extra work.

Suppose, for example, that a list of conferences visited by employees is already being maintained for other purposes anyway. Now the number of conferences at which an employee has given a presentation has been selected as an indicator. In this case, instead of going over the whole list of conferences and asking about presentations for each one at the end of each measurement cycle, one could simply add a checkbox about whether a presentation has been given to the template already being used for keeping track of conferences.

The measurement of intellectual capital also needs to be coordinated with other activities in the company. Surveys conducted by the human resources department and projects by quality assurance, for instance, frequently involve the collection of similar data. Avoiding duplicate efforts keeps costs down. Equally important, staff will be reluctant to participate in surveys if they are too frequent and too similar.

Ongoing effort

Unlike the design of a framework, which may be revised later but is expected to remain basically stable, data collection is not a one-off activity. The whole effort of measuring intellectual capital derives its value primarily from ongoing monitoring which reveals trends over time. Meaningful comparisons should not be expected before having completed at least three measurement cycles [157].

When finally writing the intellectual capital report, a point that deserves special attention is its internal consistency. Although a lot of people from different hierarchy levels may be involved in deriving indicators and in collecting the data, writing the intellectual capital report itself should involve as few people as possible.

Writing the report

Interpretation and Feedback

Once the values of the chosen indicators have been established, the time for making sense out of those numbers and reaping the benefits has finally arrived. Interpretation of the results is best accomplished in a workshop with top management. A preliminary interpretation by the project team can help to start the discussion.

The strategic model that guided the selection of indicators now also serves as a basis for discussing the results. In fact, this model should not only aid interpretation, but also help spotting actions that can be taken to deal with the issues identified. At least some of the actions should have a high degree of visibility throughout the company, since the whole initiative will quickly lose its credibility if no actions are seen to be taken in response to the results.

Interpreting the results

The discussion may also lead to a search for better indicators in some areas or reveal flaws in the strategic model itself. After several measurement cycles, the hypotheses top management holds about business success can be examined systematically by looking for corresponding trends among the values of indicators.

As an aid for interpretation, the values of the individual indicators and of whole categories of a model of intellectual capital can be aggregated [136]. Using the hierarchical structure outlined above, one would get a single value for competence, based on all the values of the indicators in that category. The same goes for the categories attitude and intellectual agility. These aggregated measures, called indices, can then in turn be aggregated into one index for human capital as a whole.

Aggregation

Indicators and categories have to be weighted so that the aggregation reflects management's views of their relative importance. The indices obtained this way will not have much meaning as absolute numbers, nor will they be particularly useful for inter-firm comparisons. They will, however, provide a good picture of relative changes over time at several different levels of abstraction.

Visualization

Categories of intellectual capital can also serve as a basis for visualizing the results of measurement. Usually, however, it is more useful to take the goals and key success factors of the strategic model as a basis for the visualization. A more ambitious approach is to construct a three-dimensional fitness landscape visualizing an aggregated intellectual capital index [88].

If target values have been established, results can also be plotted as dots in a diagram of concentric circles around the target, with the quadrants of the diagram corresponding to categories of intellectual capital and the sizes of the dots depending on the importance of the particular indicators for the company [20]. Another possibility is to use radar charts with each axis scaled separately and adjusted to have goals on the rim [155].

Providing feedback to contributors

Finally, in order to ensure the continued acceptance of the project, everyone involved in providing data should receive some feedback. This includes not only employees, but also external parties such as customers participating in a survey and partner companies providing data directly. In some cases, it may in fact be a good idea to offer compensation to external parties.

III

TECHNOLOGIES

Chapter 11

Communication

Without communication, there could be no knowledge management. This chapter takes a look at various technologies extending peoples' reach. After an overview of communication technologies, their relevance to each of the knowledge management processes is discussed. Finally, open issues and opportunities for future research and development are explored.

Overview

Communication is called synchronous if all participants engage in it at the same time, as for instance in a telephone conversation. In asynchronous communication, by contrast, participants are separated by time. An obvious example for this is communication by mail.

Synchronous, asynchronous

Many people may not perceive telephony as high-tech today, but it is still one of the most important communication technologies. Moreover, IP telephony—telephony using Internet technologies—is steadily gaining importance.

Telephony

Since this technology does not require a dedicated phone line for each conversation, calls made through IP telephony often incur significantly lower costs in the long run. IP telephony applications typically also feature a much better user interface than current telephones and better integration with other tools.

Beyond voice connections, video conferencing promises to deliver richer interaction by also displaying nonverbal cues. On the low-cost end of the spectrum, desktop video

Video conferencing

conferencing works through personal computers equipped with digital video cameras and connected via the intranet or Internet.

Professional video conferencing systems use dedicated lines and high quality voice-activated microphones to offer a guaranteed quality of service. This is the kind of system installed in boardrooms of large corporations. Prices for buying such professional solutions often run into five-digit dollar amounts. Consequently, these systems are often just rented when they are needed.

Chatrooms Chatrooms are text windows which are constantly updated to show the messages of all participating users in the order in which they were written. As new messages appear at the bottom, earlier ones are scrolled off the top. Messages are usually prefixed by the participants' names and sometimes also distinguished by different colors. Chatrooms were first conceived as entertainment applications. Only recently did they catch on for business use.

The most widespread chatroom technology on the Internet originally was IRC (Internet Relay Chat), a non-commercial, user-driven network of servers and client applications based on open standards. Nowadays, chatrooms are often hosted on web servers with Java applets running in web browsers as clients. Systems with a business focus usually either employ either such web-based chatrooms or proprietary client applications. Chatrooms can also be implemented as peer-to-peer applications, with clients communicating directly with each other rather than through a central server.

Instant messaging Originating in the consumer domain like chatrooms, instant messengers are also increasingly being used for business purposes. Instant messaging applications show a list of colleagues and indicate their status, for instance offline, online but busy, or online and available. Selecting a name lets the user send a brief text messages to that colleague.

The instant messenger of the recipient will typically be more obtrusive about the arrival of a new message than a notification about new email would be. Beyond availability awareness and messaging, many instant messengers today also offer features like initiating chat sessions with selected colleagues and sending files to them.

As the name indicates, instant messages are meant to be delivered, and also read, immediately. On the other hand, messages are also stored. Instant messaging therefore is a borderline case between synchronous and asynchronous communication.

Many mobile phones today also provide a text messaging service called SMS (short message service). This can be thought of as a kind of phone-based instant messaging, but without the ability to show the status of colleagues. Accordingly, in business settings this service is used not so much for communicating with other people, but rather to receive news items or alerts. SMS

By far the most prevalent form of asynchronous electronic communication today is email. Email is also used for a multitude of purposes beyond personal communication, for instance for group discussions and automatic alerting services. Email list management software distributes messages to lists of subscribers according to predefined sets of rules and provides administration features for those lists. Email

The need to deal with growing email archives efficiently is being addressed by email management solutions including, for example, the automatic classification of messages. Some systems enrich the content of email messages by creating links from that content to relevant portions of enterprise-wide repositories [142].

Email lists are not really convenient for conducting elaborate discussions. It is often a hassle to reconstruct the flow of arguments based on all previous messages, and since messages pertaining to different topics arrive in the order in which they were sent, users constantly need to mentally switch between topics as they get new emails from the list. Discussion forums

Electronic discussion forums, hosted on servers which automatically maintain complete archives, resolve these problems. Messages are displayed by topic and in a way which enables users to see at a glance which reply refers to which message. This is accomplished through a hierarchical structure. The topics, called threads, constitute the first level of the hierarchy. Within threads, replies are placed below the messages they refer to.

On the Internet, the original form of discussion forums are the newsgroups of Usenet, a decentralized network of servers talking to each other and to client applications. Most forums used for business purposes today are accessed through a web interface.

Audio and video messages

Asynchronous communication also includes audio and video messages. Voicemail already enjoys widespread use. In the future, multimedia messages will increasingly be sent from mobile devices, too, since those devices are typically used in circumstances in which entering text tends to be inconvenient.

Unified messaging

A drawback of using different kinds of asynchronous messaging services is that they are usually not accessible through a common interface. This dividing line is particularly pronounced between the public switched telephone network and Internet-based services.

Unified messaging enables people to manage their email, voicemail, faxes, and sometimes also other types of messaging such as SMS, in an integrated fashion. People can define rules for filtering and forwarding messages from one service to another, and messages from one service can be converted on the fly in order to be retrieved with the help of another technology.

Relevance to Knowledge Management

Communication is of crucial importance to knowledge management, and so are the technologies supporting it. The lesson learned in chapter 3 about the role of technology has been that it is important as an enabler, and communication technologies are a very good illustration for that. They are obviously not an end in themselves, but they play an essential role in enabling people to communicate and share knowledge in situations in which they could not do so without technology support.

Another lesson learned has been to leverage the power of communities. Naturally, communication technologies can make a big contribution here, for instance by providing a virtual platform like a discussion forum or mailing lists when regular face-to-face meetings are not possible. The same technologies can be very useful as a follow-up to seminars and other forms of training, allowing participants to keep in touch both with the instructor and with each other.

While these are groups of people with a lot of shared context, communication technologies are also useful for people with little shared context. Here, possibilities for rich interaction are particularly important, calling for instance for video conferencing.

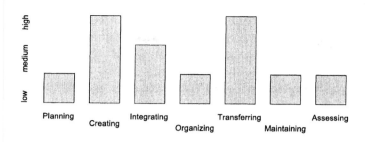

Figure 11.1. The contribution of communication technologies to the various knowledge management processes.

Communication technologies may also play a significant role in reinforcing two success factors the lessons learned have shown to be particularly important: Both a knowledge-friendly culture and employees' understanding of the knowledge management strategy can benefit from being reinforced through means like electronically delivered newsletters.

Figure 11.1 shows the extent to which communication technologies support the various knowledge management processes.

Knowledge planning usually means that a small team responsible for strategic issues sits down together, discusses, and comes to an agreement about a suitable knowledge management strategy. Communication technologies can help if some team members are not able to physically attend. On the whole, however, these technologies do not contribute a lot to knowledge planning.

Planning

Creating new knowledge, by contrast, often involves many different people from various parts of a company, and perhaps also external parties like customers, suppliers, and partners. Since stimuli arising from communication are one of the most important factors in knowledge creation, any technologies enabling more effective communication, such as instance video conferencing, are bound to have a high impact here.

Creating

Furthermore, the importance of requisite variety among the participants is well established. Communication technologies make this possible by including people who would not be able to participate otherwise. This applies to both synchronous and asynchronous communication tools. The former aid dedicated workshops, while the latter support knowledge being developed incrementally, over time, for instance through a discussion forum.

Integrating

In order to be made available to the whole company, knowledge first needs to be communicated. Both knowledge being shared by employees and knowledge being acquired from external sources will often arrive with the help of communication technologies, particularly email. Other text-based communication technologies, such as chatrooms, instant messaging, and electronic discussion forums, also lend themselves to knowledge integration, since the transcripts they produce are fairly easy to handle automatically.

Organizing

Organizing knowledge may be performed manually by individual subject matter experts, automatically, or a through a combination of both. However, it is rare that for example the classification of a particular document is achieved through a lengthy collaborative effort between many people. Therefore, communication technologies do not have much to contribute to that process.

Transferring

When it comes to tools for knowledge transfer, communication technologies are of course a natural. Whether knowledge is to be transferred in real time or asynchronously, whether one-to-one, one-to-many, or many-to-many, a range of communication technologies is available to support those activities.

The importance of this range of choices is emphasized by the lesson learned about offering multiple channels for knowledge transfer. The broad range of different communication technologies available makes it possible to choose an appropriate one based on the particular situation, the amount and type of knowledge to be transferred, and the people involved.

Transferring time-critical, context-dependent knowledge between geographically separated experts, for instance, may call for video conferencing. Real-time interactivity is essential if it is not clear in advance precisely which knowledge will be needed in order to solve a problem. By contrast, "for your information"-type current awareness knowledge will more sensibly be disseminated to many people through other communication tools such as mailing lists or discussion forums.

Maintaining knowledge, much like organizing knowledge, will seldom require a large group of people to collaborate directly. Consequently, communication technologies do not play a particularly important role here.

The assessment of knowledge often requires a lot of communication, but that is usually conducted face-to-face. Assessing knowledge therefore does not profit from communication technologies in any way particular to that process.

Maintaining

Assessing

Issues

Just because electronic means of communication are ubiquitous today, that does not mean that their use is justified under all circumstances. Email will never be able to provide the nuances of face-to-face contact, which not only serves to convey meaning more accurately, but also plays an important role in social bonding.

Email vs. face-to-face

Yet this does not imply that face-to-face meetings are always preferable to the use of communication technologies. Take the example of someone writing an email to a colleague whose office is just two doors further down the hall. This may be perfectly justified if only simple content needs to be transferred. Indeed, in that case it may be regarded as considerate towards that colleague because it does not require his immediate attention.

On the whole, electronic means of communication are generally useful for maintaining communications, but initially face-to-face meetings are preferable for getting to know each other, establishing a relationship, and building trust.

Similarly, the decision whether to use electronic discussion forums at all or stick to face-to-face meetings must not be dominated by what is technically possible.

Electronic forums vs. face-to-face

A lot of nonverbal cues will invariably be lost in online settings. This may, however, be an advantage as well as a disadvantage, as it may help to lessen the domination of a discussion by a few powerful individuals. Empirical evidence supports the claim that electronic conferencing leads to more balanced participation, more contributions from socially weaker group members, and higher influence of peripheral group members because of the omission of social and nonverbal context information [170].

Today, email is also frequently used—many would say abused—for sending files as attachments. This is one task for which email was not originally designed. People often have trouble with receiving large attachments since servers usually refuse to accept emails larger than some specified limit. That limit can be different for every server and is generally unknown to the user. In other words, one hardly ever knows how large an attachment someone's server is prepared to accept. Collaborative file management services on the Internet can solve this problem.

Problems with chatrooms

The fact that chatrooms, originally more associated with leisure pursuits rather than business, have now also been adopted by the business community, highlights their usefulness as a tool for serious work. There are, however, a number of issues which should be addressed in order to increase that usefulness.

There is no generally accepted solution to the problem of associating people with their contributions in a clear and visually intuitive way. The sense of social presence conveyed by the system would benefit from a way of indicating the difference between participants listening and writing. Turn-taking in conversations is also poorly supported. A promising approach addressing such issues seems to be threading. Familiar from asynchronous discussion forums, it can be employed in chatrooms as well [150].

Bandwidth issues

The sound quality of IP telephony conducted over the Internet is heavily dependent on the quality of the Internet connection and the amount of Internet traffic on the route of the call. With bandwidth constantly increasing and quality of service initiatives underway for Internet connections, this may not be a problem in the long run, but for now it may still result in choppy sound quality at times.

Since video requires much more bandwidth than audio, the quality of the network connection is even more critical for desktop video conferencing. In fact, however, users of desktop video conferencing often find the audio quality most irksome. This is because a picture that fails to move for a few seconds is not nearly as disruptive to the flow of communication as is an interruption of the spoken word.

Use of archives

One of the big benefits of almost all kinds of technology-based communication is that it can be archived electronically. The resulting archives can be valuable for very different purposes related to knowledge management: For the author's or recipient's own reference, for sharing with others, for optimizing the system design or configuration based on actual usage patterns, and for expertise profiling.

The latter is of course most easily accomplished with text-based tools. Emails, instant messages, discussion forum postings, and transcripts of chat sessions particularly lend themselves to that kind of analysis. The obvious issue here is which of those possibilities are actually being, or should be, used. Today, the potential offered by the use of archives of electronic forms of communication is not nearly being exploited fully.

On the other hand, considering the lessons learned about the limits of knowledge sharing and the importance of the user being in control, there are also privacy and data protection issues to be considered in developing future applications.

Keeping in mind the lesson learned about integrating different systems for knowledge management purposes, one cannot help but observe that communication technologies are often not nearly as integrated today as they could be.

Integration of technologies

Practically all telephone facilities in companies today are digital, for instance, but being able to click on a telephone number on the corporate yellow pages website and automatically being connected to the respective person is still very much the exception. Instead of being able to dial automatically from their favorite personal information management application's contact database, employees have to punch numbers into the telephone.

Furthermore, obvious features like automatic logs of all incoming and outgoing calls are missing. The problem is usually not a technological one. Solutions for this kind of integration do exist. However, they do not enjoy widespread use, which is probably at least partly due to their price.

Chapter 12

Collaboration

The first big wave of productivity applications for personal computers consisted of tools like word processors and spreadsheets, supporting individual knowledge workers. As soon as a significant fraction of those personal computers became networked, however, a new category of applications established itself: Tools supporting collaboration.

This chapter will first provide an overview of such tools, covering real-time collaboration, virtual shared spaces for groups who cannot meet at a given time, and tools supporting structured collaboration over extended periods of time. After that, the relevance of those tools to knowledge management is discussed. Finally, open issues are pointed out.

Overview

Although collaboration technologies have received a lot of attention for more than two decades now, there is still considerable disagreement over the terminology. Definitions range from the very broad (any technology improving group productivity) to the very specific (such as software for decision-making) [106]. Tools are variously referred to as groupware, CSCW (computer supported cooperative work) tools, teamware, workgroup computing applications, or simply collaboration technologies.

In this chapter, the term groupware is used for systems which provide a shared environment enabling knowledge workers to collaborate. This includes the support of geographically dispersed groups as well as groups which are separated by time. It also includes both unstructured and structured forms of collaboration.

Shared spaces   A shared space is an environment in which group members can interact. Virtual shared spaces support distributed groups by integrating communication technologies like email, discussion forums, instant messaging, chatrooms, and audio and video conferencing with further tools for real-time or asynchronous interaction. Most virtual shared spaces are hosted on servers. Increasingly, however, they are also established directly between the participants' personal computers as peer-to-peer applications.

Real-time collaboration   Shared browsing is an example for real-time interaction. It means that all the participants' web browsers automatically follow the navigation of one group member. Virtual whiteboards are used to help to explain ideas and concepts in the same way flipcharts are used in face-to-face meetings.

Idea collection   Idea collection tools make brainstorming possible for dispersed groups. In brainstorming, the focus is on the quantity and breadth of the ideas generated, not on their relationships. When those ideas are collected with an appropriate tool, however, they are captured in a form in which they can easily be structured with further groupware components such as collaborative outliners or concept mapping tools.

Collaborative writing   Collaborative writing would seem to be another obvious candidate. So far, however, real-time collaborative work on documents has not taken on as a mainstream application. This kind of work is usually conducted asynchronously. A number of problems still plague synchronous computer supported collaborative writing [30].

Asynchronous collaboration   Collaborative writing, brainstorming, and outlining can of course also be conducted asynchronously. Asynchronous brainstorming is of particular interest here, since brainstorming typically benefits from large groups with the requisite variety for collecting interesting contributions. Asynchronous electronic brainstorming in very large groups can be conducted in two ways: Either by letting every subgroup start from scratch, or by letting every next subgroup build on the results from the previous subgroup. The latter approach was found not only to be more productive, but also to lead to greater participant satisfaction [42].

File sharing   Shared file archives have long been a standard component of groupware systems. These archives usually do not offer the sophistication of fully-fledged document management solutions. Their aim is to enable quick sharing of existing information within the group without sidetracking the user, and they are kept accordingly simple.

A feature gaining more and more popularity among mainstream products are electronic polls. These voting mechanisms can not only be used as components in their own right, but may be functionally integrated with other components

Voting mechanisms

Each message in a discussion forum, for instance, may automatically be equipped with a facility for the reader to rate this contribution. The data collected in this way may be used both for filtering messages based on the ratings and for creating a profile of the reader's interests or expertise.

Organizational information management application like shared task lists, calendars, address books, and bookmark collections complement the offering of shared spaces. Again, the level of sophistication of these tools varies widely.

Collaborative organizing

Task management can be anything from a simple to-do list to a complete project management solution. Calendars often support the automated allocation of time slots not just for people, but also for the resources they need, such as meeting rooms. Address books may be connected to corporate yellow pages or customer databases.

Finally, a somewhat atypical example of asynchronous shared spaces are wiki webs and similar systems. These are web servers on which any content can be edited via the web by anybody, anytime. Usually focused on a particular theme, the content of many of these systems has evolved surprisingly well even if they were open for editing by literally everybody on the Internet.

Wiki webs

Systems tailored specifically to the support of face-to-face meetings rather than distributed groups are commonly referred to as group support systems. In the simplest case, such systems might just consist of a video projector connected to a notebook computer running appropriate software. A fully-fledged version would include separate keyboards for all participants or link all their notebooks and handhelds. These would be connected to a server which also takes care of a generally visible projected display.

Group support systems

Projecting the contents of a computer screen on the wall is not the end of the story, however. There are already smart walls allowing direct interaction with objects on the wall, as well as technologies for three-dimensional projections. Furthermore, depending on the task to be accomplished, group support systems employ special software, for instance group decision support systems.

Workflow management

The collaboration technologies discussed so far excel at supporting largely unstructured kinds of collaboration. If, however, the tasks to be accomplished typically involve recurring patterns, such as in insurance claims processing or the editorial review process of a periodical, other approaches are called for.

This is where workflow management systems come into play. They manage the automation of business process according to sets of rules, passing content and tasks from one participant to another for action [177].

Workflow management systems generally consist of several components. First the relevant processes have to be modeled. This is primarily an analytical task performed by experts, but is usually supported by some form of workflow editing tool. Many workflow management systems also include tools allowing the modeled workflow to be simulated before the actual rollout in the organization. A workflow engine interprets and enacts the rules established in the modeling phase, thus forming the core of the workflow management system. Finally, a monitoring component allows keeping track of the actual use of the system and can provide valuable statistics like lead times to management.

Relevance to Knowledge Management

Groupware systems are typically suites of applications focused on supporting collaboration by enabling knowledge sharing and fostering communication among group members. As such, these systems have an obvious role as enablers of knowledge management. Since groupware environments provide rich communications facilities, the benefits of communication technologies for knowledge management, as discussed in the previous chapter, also apply to groupware. But because of the integrated nature of groupware environments and the range of applications they support, their value for knowledge management is even greater.

For example, shared spaces not only make meetings of geographically dispersed employees possible, but by integrating communication technologies like video conferenc-

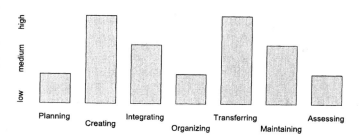

Figure 12.1. The contribution of collaboration technologies to the various knowledge management processes.

ing with other features like virtual whiteboards and shared browsing, they add a new quality to those meetings.

Furthermore, groupware systems not only enable knowledge management through the content that passes through them, but also through the structure these systems exhibit. Shared spaces, for instance, may incorporate distinct areas for content related to different projects or persons, and workflow management systems embody a wealth of knowledge about the business processes of an organization.

One of the biggest challenges in knowledge management, as the lessons learned in chapter 3 have shown, is to create a knowledge sharing culture, to dispel fears that sharing knowledge will lead to loss of power, that nothing will ever come back in return. Groupware environments, provided of course they are designed appropriately, can help by making reciprocity more visible. Since they support groups over a considerable length of time and with a range of tools for performing different tasks, they have more leverage here than stand-alone tools.

Figure 12.1 shows the extent to which collaboration technologies support the various knowledge management processes.

Knowledge planning is not supported by collaboration technologies in any way particular to that process. While such tools may of course be used in that context, they are unlikely to add a lot of value.

Knowledge creation, by contrast, may benefit enormously from virtual shared spaces, particularly if features such as electronic brainstorming and whiteboarding are supported.

Compared to face-to-face brainstorming, the electronic version has one important advantage: Contributions can be anonymous, which may significantly reduce the inhibition threshold of the participants and therefore help to collect not only more ideas, but also more innovative ones.

With the help of group support systems, this effect can also be leveraged in face-to-face meetings. Particular benefits of group support systems for knowledge creation include larger effective group sizes, the reduction of idea production blocking through the need to listen to the ideas of others, and support for process structuring [19]. Experimental studies have also shown group support systems to positively impact knowledge creation in focus groups [126].

Taking a more general view, shared spaces often focus on a particular subject, theme, or project, while still being fairly unstructured and supporting multiple forms of communication. This kind of environment is inherently more conducive to the generation of new knowledge than working with, for example, a classical document management system.

Integrating

Knowledge integration stands to benefit from collaboration technologies in at least two ways. First, groupware environments allow users to capture knowledge gained from the group in the context of their work and communication.

Second, knowledge contributed to the group will not only be available to other group members, but will be more integrated in the mind of the author too: The process of contributing itself establishes a new context. There is also empirical evidence for the benefits of group support systems to both individual knowledge acquisition and collaborative learning [95].

Organizing

Organizing knowledge is usually either performed by individual human experts (rather than a group collaboratively handling the same content) or completely automated. Collaboration technologies therefore have little to offer in support of that process.

Transferring

Knowledge transfer means communication of knowledge, and this is of course an area in which groupware applications excel. Because of the wide variety of synchronous and asynchronous facilities they provide with a common user interface, groupware systems make it easy to switch between different modes of knowledge transfer depending on the purpose and urgency of the task at hand. Workflow management systems support knowledge transfer not only by routing relevant knowledge, but also through the management of deadlines and alerts.

Knowledge maintenance is supported primarily by workflow components, for instance by handling editorial processes. However, shared spaces may also play an important role. Since they foster communication, particularly among geographically dispersed groups, these systems may indirectly lead to the identification of outdated knowledge at an early stage.

Knowledge assessment, like knowledge planning, is a process generally conducted at the strategic level. Groupware environments will typically not have much of an impact on this process.

Issues

Knowledge has to be structured, as one lesson learned has pointed out. At first sight, this seems to be a bit at odds with the way shared spaces are usually used: They are typically targeted at informal, unstructured collaboration. Knowledge contained in shared spaces generally takes the form of, for example, unstructured files being shared or unstructured chat transcripts.

Structure in shared spaces

While all of this is true, it does not mean that no structure can be discerned in the total body of knowledge contained in the system. Different types of knowledge, for instance, will naturally appear in different forms like shared documents or chat transcripts. These forms may thus act as a sort of categories in themselves even if they were not originally conceived as such. Nevertheless, more support for dedicated structural elements than is typically being offered by today's systems would be desirable.

On the organizational side, the issue is to find a suitable balance between emphasizing structure in order to foster eventual knowledge reuse on the one hand and providing the required degrees of freedom for informal collaboration on the other.

Another lesson learned has highlighted the importance of integrating existing systems into new solutions. In the case of groupware, this means that communication tools such as email have to be integrated into a comprehensive suite of applications with a uniform user interface.

Integrating existing tools

This challenge is not just a technical one: Once a groupware system is rolled out, for example, employees are usually expected to conduct all their email correspondence through that system rather than their old email client, to which some may have become quite attached.

Open standards On the technical side, problems may arise with the integration of tools that are not based on open standards. Instant messengers are a case in point: Although efforts to standardize instant messaging protocols have been underway for quite some time, most of the widespread tools still use their own proprietary protocols.

Ideally, groupware systems would also integrate phone and fax services. If file sharing is a priority and a document management solution is already being used in the company, that system should be integrated into the groupware environment as well.

Promoting trust The importance of promoting trust among employees has been emphasized by another lesson learned. Up to a point, collaboration technologies support this by helping geographically dispersed employees to get to "know" each other at least virtually, but in a more comprehensive fashion than would be possible, say, only through telephone calls.

However, current groupware systems are generally designed for maximizing the efficiency of collaboration and do not pay much attention to issues of trust between group members. While this is, of course, perfectly reasonable for some applications, there are others which would benefit from systems designed differently.

Pilot projects That any major knowledge management initiative should start with a pilot project has also been a lesson learned. In many respects, groupware is an obvious candidate for starting such a project: The focus can be on one particular group in a natural way. The front-end usually makes sense to users who are already familiar with components like calendars, contact lists, and communication tools. Any added knowledge management functionality may not be so prominent at first sight, which decreases the danger of users shying away because of that. Finally, many groupware components can be used right out of the box, reducing the time and the budget necessary for the pilot.

The danger here is that precisely because groupware seems such an obvious choice to start a knowledge management initiative with, one might be tempted to introduce it in a pilot even though problems addressed by other solutions really are more pressing. Another lesson learned is pertinent here: Knowledge management has to address real needs.

Finally, the lesson learned about the limits of knowledge sharing also raises some issues for collaboration technologies. On the technical side, there have to be mechanisms for managing access rights on a suitable level of granularity. In particular, there should not only be a distinction between different groups, but also a possibility for users to mark some items as completely private. This makes it possible for employees to maintain for instance their personal calendars in the groupware system as well, rather than in a separate application. The importance of factors like this for the acceptance of new systems must not be underestimated.

Access rights

On the organizational side, the question of who should belong to which groups becomes more prominent than in informal networking between people, where a clear distinction between belonging or not belonging to a group is often not possible, nor would it be necessary. Collaboration technologies, by contrast, require the administrator to precisely define group memberships, and everybody will be aware which groups they are being considered part of—or not. Furthermore, decisions about group membership should also take into account the fact that interpreting and understanding content contributed by others often requires a shared mental frame of reference [86].

Group membership

Chapter 13

Content Creation

Specialized tools enable the creation of various kinds of content ranging from text documents to expertise profiles. This chapter provides an overview of such tools, discusses their relevance to knowledge management, and points out issues arising in the context of their use.

Overview

The most obvious instruments for content creation are authoring tools. General-purpose word processors as well as a plethora of applications for more specialized tasks, such as writing technical documentation or designing web pages, focus mainly on the creation of text and layout. Dedicated multimedia authoring tools, by contrast, permit the creation of graphics and sounds, as well as their arrangement in animated sequences involving user interaction. Advanced authoring solutions also support the collaboration of several authors working on the same documents.

Authoring tools

Annotation technologies support the creation of another kind of content: Not large documents, but short comments or notes attached to documents or parts of them. Currently mainly used for text, annotation facilities are increasingly becoming available for multimedia content as well.

Annotations

Annotations may be private, visible only to their author, or they may be public. In the latter case, some advanced systems also support replies, with the original annotation effectively serving as the starting point for a threaded discussion. When using standalone tools like word processors with annotation features, annotations are embedded in the original document. Online services catering for many users simultaneously store annotations in separate databases.

Stimulating creativity

The range of tools supporting content creation is not restricted to applications allowing people to explicate their existing knowledge. It also includes tools meant to stimulate creativity. One popular method is to provide random words, short texts, and pictures from a suitable pre-selected collection at the right time. Another approach is to have a tool come up with intelligent questions guiding the user through the task at hand, dynamically adapted to the user's input and actions so far.

Handling structure

Beyond content in the narrower sense, such as texts and pictures, the structures used to organize knowledge that have been discussed in chapter 7 are a kind of content in their own right. Sophisticated tools are available for creating and maintaining large classification schemes and thesauri. Ontology editors are perhaps the most versatile tools in this category, although that power is often bought at the expense of ease of use. Other tools focusing on creating structural content deal with navigation facilities, both within documents and within large collections or websites. Particularly helpful are solutions that combine authoring capabilities with advanced structuring functionality.

Document enrichment

Content creation consists not just of creating new documents from scratch, but also of enriching existing documents. First, the value of documents can be increased by making them more amenable to further processing: Optical character recognition and speech recognition software convert images and audio into text files. Value can also be added by interlinking and adding metadata.

Up to a point, document enrichment can be automated. Advanced systems employ statistical methods, artificial intelligence, and collaborative filtering, drawing on both content and usage data in order to automatically link documents to similar ones, or to assign keywords or other metadata to those documents. While the quality of the results will generally not be as high as that of documents enriched manually by skilled professionals, it may be more than sufficient for practical use.

The big advantage of an automated approach lies in the volume of content that can be processed in a very short time.

For small collections, the initial investment required will not be justified, and many of the methods employed by these systems only work well with huge numbers of documents anyway. For large repositories, however, both the time and the expenses incurred by document enrichment may be lowered dramatically through automation.

One kind of content is a particularly tempting target for automated approaches to content creation: Information about who in the company possesses what kinds of expertise. The motivation for trying to automate the building of expertise profiles is not just one of efficiency, but also one of accuracy, since the judgment of superiors, peers, and employees themselves often turns out to be unreliable. Expertise profiling software cannot work wonders either, of course, but it can avoid some of the biases people tend to succumb to.

Since so much information is being kept electronically today, there is a wide range of sources that lend themselves to being analyzed by expertise profiling systems. First, there are intranet sites and document repositories. Their usage statistics and metadata show who has authored or collected which documents. Then there are records of various forms of communication: Archives and server log files of email, instant messages, and discussion forums, telephone connection data, and meeting minutes all show who has communicated with whom, and often also on what subject. Web browsing histories and bookmarks, as well as queries sent to Internet or intranet search engines and databases, provide detailed information on individual interests and probable expertise. Subscriptions to periodicals, visits to conferences and trade fairs, and the projects employees have been involved in complete the picture.

Expertise profiling

More generally, the term data mining is used for the automated creation of new content by identifying patterns in existing data. Data mining methods again range from statistical techniques to artificial intelligence. Unlike document enrichment and expertise profiling, data mining efforts often focus on analyzing large quantities of numerical data.

Data mining

Relevance to Knowledge Management

The importance of content creation technologies for knowledge management stems not only from the obvious fact that they are essential in enabling employees to explicate knowl-

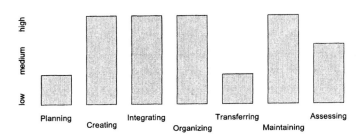

Figure 13.1. The contribution of content creation technologies to the various knowledge management processes.

edge efficiently. It also derives from the fact that some of those tools support collaborative authoring by a group of people. That process may in itself be a valuable way of learning and sharing knowledge among the different authors. In other words, advanced authoring solutions today directly support the lesson learned in chapter 3 to promote collaboration.

Expertise profiling helps to address several further lessons learned. First, there is the lesson that knowledge management should be embedded in work processes. Now expertise profiling obviously is as embedded as it gets, since such systems can operate in the background without disrupting the work of employees.

Second, there is the lesson to pay attention to tacit knowledge. Expertise profiling may reveal such tacit knowledge, for instance by discovering that someone is constantly being emailed with requests for help or advice on a particular topic even though he has never authored and thereby explicated any document on that topic.

Finally, there is the lesson to leverage the power of communities. In this context, expertise profiling may help to identify potential future communities, the members of which have not been aware of their common interests so far.

Figure 13.1 shows the extent to which content creation technologies support the various knowledge management processes.

Tools for content creation will have to be considered in planning, but they do not themselves directly contribute to that process in any significant way.

While most knowledge creation happens in the heads of individuals, some of it can also be automated. Expertise profiling, through analyzing available information about employees, may generate new knowledge about the distribution of expertise in the organization which was hitherto neither available electronically nor known by any employees. Document enrichment technologies can be used to automatically link related items in a corporate repository and to add relevant metadata to those items, thereby creating contextualized content. Furthermore, tools designed to stimulate the creativity of authors positively impact knowledge creation.

Creating

In spite of commonly being called knowledge creation tools, the real purpose of all sorts of authoring tools is not so much the actual creation of knowledge, which really happens in the minds of the users of such tools, but to capture and store that knowledge, to integrate it with the pool of knowledge directly available to the company at large. Similarly, data mining is mainly about identifying knowledge that is hidden in some repository. Through data mining, that knowledge is made explicit and available for the organization.

Integrating

Authoring tools that try to identify content in the repository that is similar to the one currently being authored may not only make it easier for the author to link to other relevant items, but also, and perhaps more importantly, help people to get a feeling for what is already available in a given context and at what level. In a well-developed repository, this may be a good indicator for what is valuable to others in the company, thereby helping the author to focus on packaging the most relevant knowledge.

Good authoring tools also allow people to express themselves with a minimum of effort. Since people often would not contribute their new knowledge to a repository if it was too much of a hassle, this is again a very good example for the lesson learned about the enabling role of technology in knowledge management.

Another lesson learned has addressed the difficulty of filling a repository with appropriate content. Here, efficient content creation technologies can help by significantly lowering the costs of the particularly problematic initial seeding of the repository.

Modern authoring tools not only allow users to create unstructured content like text documents. Rather, they also support the management of metadata and structural elements. There is a whole class of applications developed specifi-

Organizing

cally for creating and managing structures like classification schemes. Organizing knowledge therefore stands to gain a lot from content creation technologies, both in terms of handling specific items of content and in terms of dealing with the overall structure of a repository.

Transferring

The kinds of tools discussed in this chapter help with creating new content, but they do not directly support the process of actually communicating the knowledge contained in that content to other employees.

Maintaining

Content maintenance, by contrast, will often make use of the same tools that were originally used to create the content in question. This applies to both authoring tools and technologies for the automated creation of content. The latter, in particular, will typically be used to constantly update content like expertise profiles. Indeed, that is one of the main attractions of that kind of technology: Being fully automated, content creation and updates are not limited to the times when employees can take care of them.

Assessing

Tools creating new content automatically based on authorship of existing content are in a good position to support the assessment of the knowledge of an organization. Expertise profiling may sometimes even infer tacit knowledge held by employees.

Ideally, there will be a feedback loop between expertise profiling and general knowledge assessment, but not only that: One of the lessons learned has been to integrate knowledge management measures with training, so the feedback loop should also extend to that.

Issues

Availability and selection of suitable tools

A lesson learned has highlighted importance of properly understanding the knowledge requirements of an organization. Addressing this not only includes creating the right content, but also using content creation tools the right way and selecting the right tools in the first place.

If the knowledge management strategy emphasizes dealing with the structure of documents, for instance, tools that do not adequately support structured content will not be of much use. Promoting the actual use of available knowledge, which has been another of the lessons learned, will also benefit from tools supporting structure, as they often make users more aware of what else is available. The main issues here are, therefore, the availability and the selection of suitable tools.

Ideally, users of authoring tools will be able to include elements that already exist in a repository in a simple and intuitive way. For example, the repository may contain objects representing persons, projects, and documents, and the user might want to put a reference to a project into the document he is just authoring.

Accessing repositories

This should be possible in a more intuitive way than copying a URL (uniform resource locator) into the text. The user should be able to browse the repository in a way that makes full use of that repository's features, such as filtering according to types of objects, from within the authoring tool, and to select the object of interest to him there.

This will require the authoring tool to understand the way the repository operates and is organized. Today's solutions, however, are typically standalone tools used for editing and uploading single documents without being able to make use of the advanced features of modern repositories or the structure of content beyond the currently edited document. A tighter integration would be most welcome here.

Having appropriate tools at one's disposal is not enough, however. Authoring tools may be powerful, but that power will be lost unless the users of those tools are able to employ them properly. This is yet another incarnation of the lesson learned about the need to develop knowledge skills. Leveraging the power of modern authoring tools is one such skill.

Authoring skills

Experience shows that even in comparatively simple tools like word processors, basic features that have been around for many years are often still not being used. Distinguishing headlines by increasing their font size instead of assigning the proper paragraph style still is a frequently found example. Obviously, building the necessary skills is particularly important if authoring tools are to be used by employees in general, rather than just by content creation specialists.

While quite a lot of research has been carried out on what makes documents good and usable, most of the results are unfortunately not widely known, particularly when it comes to writing for online resources such as websites that are typically browsed rather than read in depth. Authoring tools can compensate this up to a point by providing templates that have been designed not only with visual appeal in mind, but also with a view to the usability of the resulting documents.

Privacy issues   Finally, expertise profiling poses serious privacy issues. Not everything that is technically possible when analyzing data like email correspondence and web surfing habits of employees will be deemed acceptable or even legal in many countries. Some systems give users near total control over the extent to which any personal information will be shared with others. However, very little is known yet about precisely where to best draw the line in order to maximize benefits to both the company and the individual employee without violating anyone's rights or sense of privacy.

Chapter 14

Content Management

The idea behind both content management systems and document management systems is to support the management of pieces of information over their whole lifecycle. While document management systems deal with complete documents, content management systems typically handle smaller chunks of information which are then joined together as needed. The focus of document management is primarily on providing efficient access to existing documents rather than on manipulating what is inside of those documents. Content management is also concerned with creating and editing smaller pieces of content, and with dynamically creating documents from those pieces.

Content management and document management

Many features are therefore common to both kinds of systems, and indeed there is a recognizable trend of convergence in available products. Enterprise content management can be regarded as the more general concept, including elements of both document management and web content management. This chapter first provides an overview of the major functions of such systems, followed by the discussion of their relevance to knowledge management. Finally, issues to be addressed in future implementations are considered.

Overview

Existing paper documents are brought into content management systems through scanning. Optical character recognition software analyzes the resulting images files and translates them into computer-readable text. Content that is al-

Merging content

ready available electronically, for instance in the form of word processor files, may pass through conversion filters before being absorbed into the repository.

Many content management systems also provide authoring components. Templates support the creation of new items. An overview of different kinds of authoring tools can be found in chapter 13.

Metadata   One of the most important features of all content management systems is the management of metadata. Metadata provide additional information about pieces of content. Typical attributes would be the author, keywords describing the content, and the dates of an item's creation, review, and approval. Metadata may also include quality ratings and annotations by users.

Storage   Both the content itself and the metadata associated with it are stored in a database in order to permit efficient retrieval. In addition, many content management systems feature interfaces to external sources of content such as production databases or newsfeeds.

Versioning   Versioning is the ability to automatically keep track of different versions of documents. Whenever a document is checked out for editing, it is locked on the server so no one else can modify it at the same time. This permits groups to safely collaborate on documents. When a new version is saved back to the system, it is stored along with the old one, but with an incremented version number. A roll-back to a previous version is therefore always possible. Versioning also satisfies audit trail requirements.

Classification   From the user's point of view, easy access to content not only means quickly getting content once it is located, but also being able to locate it easily in the first place. For this reason, many document management systems support the structuring of collections, for instance through classification schemes. Leading-edge systems offer both clustering to automatically generate suitable categories and the automated classification of documents into those categories.

Link management   Content management systems typically approach the task of structuring with a site management component with which the overall navigation model can be established. A link management component ensures that the targets of all links are valid. If an item is moved, for example, all links pointing to it will automatically be changed as well.

Retrieval facilities have to support two different kinds of tasks: Locating known content and finding hitherto unknown content on a given subject. The criteria determining the quality of the content retrieved are precision and recall. Precision means that all items that are retrieved should be relevant. Recall refers to the other obvious demand: That all relevant items should actually be retrieved.

Content management systems usually maintain an index of the text of all documents as well as of their associated metadata. This ensures adequate performance of search technologies ranging from simple Boolean searching (using operators like "and", "or", "not") to more advanced tools employing natural language processing [55] and context specific term weighting [54]. Thesauri and algorithms for query reformulation help to increase the quality of search queries, and consequently of the results retrieved. Furthermore, searchers may also benefit from being able to use past queries of other people [93].

The retrieval of multimedia content requires specialized approaches. Images can be retrieved either through a description of the features of the images sought, or based on their similarity to a given image. Progress is also being made with the retrieval of audio and video content [171].

Unlike document management systems, which simply provide documents as they are, content management systems separate layout from content. Depending on the context, an output template containing formatting instructions is selected and used to assemble various pieces of content into a document on demand.

Workflow management, already described in chapter 12, can also be a component of content management systems. A typical application would support the editorial process: The submission of a draft, its review, and its approval leading to its publication.

Finally, most content management systems support a role-based security model. Apart from protecting sensitive information, this also allows responsibilities for maintaining certain areas of content to be devolved in a controlled fashion. Authentication is not always handled by the system itself: Major systems eliminate the need for administrating separate user accounts by providing interfaces to existing directory services.

Margin notes:
Retrieval

Output

Workflow

Security

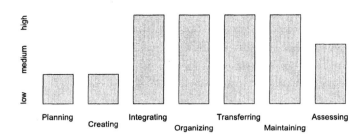

Figure 14.1. The contribution of content management technologies to the various knowledge management processes.

Relevance to Knowledge Management

Most of the explicit knowledge of a company is laid down in some type of document. Any technology helping to manage all those documents will therefore play an important role for a comprehensive knowledge management effort. Content management systems typically also satisfy the requirements raised by two of the lessons learned in chapter 3: That knowledge has to be structured, and that knowledge management tasks should be embedded in work processes that are being carried out anyway. The former is met by elaborate functionalities for classification and for dealing with metadata, and the latter by systems integrating themselves into common office applications like word processors.

Figure 14.1 shows the extent to which content management technologies support the various knowledge management processes.

Knowledge planning, as a decision-making activity firmly set on the strategic level, usually will not benefit a lot from this kind of systems. Their contribution is only an indirect one, by making documented knowledge relevant to decision-making processes readily available.

The situation is similar for the creation of new knowledge, which will of course often be based on existing knowledge. Content management systems may make access to such documented background knowledge easier, but they do not directly support the core activities of creating knowledge.

By contrast, content management systems are highly relevant to integrating knowledge. Employees who explicate some of their knowledge to make it available to the entire organization will typically do so by writing down what they know, drawing a diagram, or selecting good references for a given subject. In short, they are creating pieces of content which can be made available to others in an efficient manner through appropriate systems.

Document management systems also help with organizing knowledge by supporting the classification of documents. More generally, content management systems excel at dealing with all kinds of metadata.

Organizing

Because of their sophisticated retrieval facilities, such systems constitute an invaluable tool for transferring knowledge. Advanced search capabilities enable experts to conduct highly efficient searches, while the ability to handle natural language queries enables a larger audience to benefit from the transfer of documented knowledge.

Transferring

The maintenance of knowledge particularly benefits from features like automated versioning and archiving, but also from the good support of metadata, which may for instance be used to set expiry dates for certain items of content.

Maintaining

While the assessment of knowledge is often primarily conducted on the strategic level, content management systems may help to some extent if they support classification and the rating of content by users. Analysis may show, for example, that a lot of content exist in a strategically important area, but that none of it has been rated as particularly useful by employees.

Assessing

Issues

How can systems handle relationships between documents? The standard answers are through interlinking and through classification. However, large collections of documents with a high number of links between them, as they are typically used today, may cause considerable confusion among users.

Using different types of links

An alternative would be to introduce different types of links denoting different types of relationships between documents. Together with a suitable way of displaying these different types of links, this would enable users to distinguish between the different meanings of links and to selectively follow only the more relevant ones. Unfortunately, this approach also increases the cognitive load on the user, who now has to keep in mind all the different types of links. Overall, there seems to be no general guideline for deciding when it makes sense to use typed links. For systems design, this implies that it might be a good idea to support them just in case.

Maintaining classification schemes

The other major approach to imposing structure on a given collection of documents, the use of classification schemes, also suffers some open issues, particularly when it comes to maintaining those classification schemes. Attempting to completely automate that maintenance may ultimately prove to be an elusive goal. However, significant advancements have been made in adjusting categories through automated category decomposition and category merging based on an existing set of categories and the documents associated with them [173].

Another problem related to the maintenance of classification schemes is that changes to the category structure often interfere with users' understanding of a given document collection. This problem has been approached from an angle emphasizing the collaborative management of categories [48].

Dealing with context

An open issue in retrieving content that is especially important for knowledge management lies in how to best deal with the context of the query. Possible approaches include relevance feedback, user profiles, word-sense disambiguation, and symbolic user modeling. A state-of-the art system observes how users interact with common applications and is then able to anticipate users' needs [26].

These are promising developments, but there is still ample room for future research on how to take context into account. In particular, it is still quite unclear which technology is the most appropriate one for which kind of situation. An engineer retrieving technical documentation while carrying out routine aircraft maintenance, and a senior manager retrieving reports for the purpose of crafting a business strategy, for instance, will not draw the same benefits from the same tools.

Limiting content

At first sight, it may appear that in the ideal case, all the documented knowledge of a company will automatically find its way into one central system. In practice, however, there is the real danger of cluttering the system with useless information and ending up with a knowledge junkyard instead of a pool of content relevant to business. Three lessons learned should be kept in mind here: Understand the knowledge requirements, use technology only to address real needs, and promote the actual use of knowledge.

Appropriate retrieval capabilities are important here, since without them available knowledge will not get used. Considering only retrieval is not enough, however. Even the best retrieval technologies will perform poorly when they have to deal with a knowledge junkyard. Often, a decision will be called for to limit the content of a repository to certain types. Achieving an appropriate balance can be quite a challenge.

Finally, content management systems will often need to access legacy systems or supersede them. In either case, advanced capabilities offered by the new system will either have to be learned by users or go unused. Since not every feature is important for every user, there is a real choice here.

Legacy systems

This issue may also occur in a slightly less problematic form: Capabilities may be roughly the same, but the user interface may differ. The retrieval components of various content management systems, for example, use different conventions for query formulation. The issue here is to decide either to educate users about the new search syntax, and in which form to do so, or to try to customize the system by implementing a query reformulation module that translates users' old-style queries into the new syntax.

Chapter 15

Adaptation

Adaptation technologies deal with tailoring content to particular users or groups of users. On the one hand, they are concerned with selecting and reformatting content for certain tasks. On the other hand, these technologies offer choices for rendering that content in a way appropriate to the target audience. This chapter briefly surveys such technologies, discusses their relevance to knowledge management, and points out related issues.

Overview

Two basic approaches to adapting content can be distinguished: Customization and personalization. There is some confusion about the meaning of those two terms. Here, customization refers to choices that are under direct user control. Users explicitly communicate their preferences to the system, which from then on delivers content according to their wishes.

Personalization, by contrast, is about predicting users' needs. This may take the form of an administrator describing other users' interests, or it may involve the system itself observing the behavior of users and inferring their preferences. While customization makes content adaptable, personalization makes it adaptive.

From a technological point of view, personalization is more challenging than customization. If the two approaches appear to be in conflict with each other, however, that is usually a question of policy rather than of technology: Who should have what level of control over content delivery? And how much effort should they have to invest? Many technologies can be used in connection with either approach.

Recommender systems

In order to present only the most relevant content to the user, recommender systems maintain profiles of their users. In most cases, these profiles are not directly specified by people, but instead are constructed by the system based on how useful people find various items of content. To that end, users may be asked to rate documents they have been using in the past, or the system may unobtrusively observe what kinds of documents users access and infer peoples' interests.

Recommender systems are of particular interest if they do not only analyze direct connections between users and content, but also match user profiles. This way, the system can recommend content to a user based on what other users with similar interests have found useful in the past. The power of this kind of collaborative filtering lies in the fact that it relies less on the system's capabilities for inferring preferences. Instead, it leverages human judgment to a greater extent. Collaborative filtering will, however, only work well when a large number of users is involved.

Document adaptation

Once it is clear which documents should find their way to the user, the content of those documents can be adapted as well. Possibilities range from simply removing irrelevant parts, such as advertisements on web pages, to applying sophisticated methods of text analysis, for instance to automatically summarize the content of documents. The most advanced of such methods employ artificial intelligence techniques and are therefore discussed in more detail in chapter 18.

Data warehousing

Data warehousing is an example of adapting content for further processing in a way that is often invisible to the end user. A data warehouse pulls together great amounts of content from different operational databases, reformats that data in a consistent manner, and stores it in a dedicated repository. It is this repository, rather than the original databases, which is then used for purposes of business analysis.

Portals

The purpose of portals is also to draw together content from various sources. The focus here is on the user interface, however. Ideally, portals aggregate and present both structured and unstructured content in a way geared not only to users' information needs, but also their work processes.

Accordingly, portals can be designed not only for generally staying informed, but also for tasks like collaboration and decision-making.

A picture often says more than a thousand words. Per- **Visualization**
haps even more importantly, however, it is usually also much easier to interpret. People are very quick at picking up patterns in images. Visualization technologies make use of this fact by displaying content in a way tailored to the strengths of the human perceptual system. A wide range of both two-dimensional and three-dimensional visualization methods are available for numerical data as well as logical structures like hierarchies and networks.

Visualizations specifically designed to depict knowledge **Knowledge**
structures, knowledge sources, or knowledge flows are often **maps**
referred to as knowledge maps. Creating knowledge maps does not necessarily require any special technologies. Producing many different knowledge maps tailored to particular employees and situations, however, will only be a realistic proposition if at least part of the process is automated.

Relevance to Knowledge Management

The very first and most important lesson learned in chapter 3 has been that knowledge management must always be primarily about people. The mandate of technology, then, becomes to help people in a way that does not require them to adapt to tools any more than absolutely necessary; rather, technology should adapt itself to its users. This is precisely what is being offered by technologies for the adaptation of knowledge. They make it possible to tailor both what people see and how they see it to each particular user.

One example is to display not just the content in question, but to also show ratings assigned to that content by users. This may help with an issue raised by another lesson learned: Promoting trust. On the one hand, such ratings may increase the trust people have in highly rated content. On the other hand, the ability to assign ratings themselves may also increase the trust people have in the overall system.

It is also important to keep in mind that in the real world, decisions are not being made on a purely rational basis. Technologies presenting knowledge in a visually appealing way can be very impressive, much more so than abstract talk about, say, the relative merits of one particular algorithm

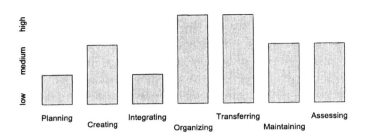

Figure 15.1. The contribution of adaptation technologies to the various knowledge management processes.

over another for a given task. It would not be the first time that this fact has been exploited in order to obtain buy-in from top management or employees.

Figure 15.1 shows the extent to which adaptation technologies support the various knowledge management processes.

Knowledge planning does not benefit a lot. Only visualization techniques can make a modest contribution by displaying pertinent information, for instance about knowledge gaps, in a more intuitive way.

Although adaptation technologies primarily benefit the efficient use of existing knowledge, some such tools also help with the creation of new knowledge. Various visualization methods, in particular, have proven their worth in fostering creativity by making it easier to discern relationships. They can make underlying assumptions more visible and encourage viewing matters from alternative perspectives.

Personalization technologies are usually used to adapt content in a way that fits in well with the mental model of the target user. In fostering creativity, however, it is often useful to encourage out-of-the-box thinking by confronting people with things that are as far away as possible from their usual thinking habits. For this purpose, the same user profiles that already exist for personalization may be employed, and the very same technology that is more commonly used to provide good fits might be employed to stimulate creative thinking by sometimes providing deliberately "bad" fits.

The technologies discussed in this chapter are concerned with the adaptation of knowledge that is already available the organization, whereas integrating knowledge is all about making knowledge available. Consequently, these technologies are of little relevance to the integration of knowledge.

Organizing knowledge, by contrast, benefits from these technologies in a big way. Visualization can help tremendously both to structure knowledge itself and to help others understand a structure once it is established. For example, complex multidimensional visualizations based on metadata and extracted key terms may be used in order to determine a useful but simpler structure for a collection of documents. The resulting structure may then take the form of a knowledge map which is immediately intelligible to all employees concerned.

Recommender systems, too, are not only useful for ad-hoc recommendations to individuals. They also support the organization of knowledge for particular groups of people with similar interests. This not only means the production of, say, specific knowledge maps targeted at those groups, but also identifying those groups in the first place. Since groups with similar interests cannot always be readily inferred from organizational attributes like job title, department, and involvement in projects, the user profiles generated by recommender systems may be a valuable help here.

In situations where a picture says more than a thousand words, knowledge transfer obviously benefits from visualization technologies. Well-designed portals also facilitate the transfer of knowledge, both by making it easier to access content from different sources and by selectively pointing to particularly relevant content. Perhaps the most important technologies here, however, are personalization and recommender systems. They bring content that probably ought to be transferred to the attention of users—content whose existence or relevance may not have been realized by either the user or the administrator of a run-of-the-mill portal.

Knowledge maintenance may not exactly depend on technologies discussed in this chapter, but it can certainly benefit from them. This can be as simple as making sure that the date of the last modification is always shown with each item of content. Maintainers of large repositories will find various methods of visualizing hierarchies and networks helpful. In fact, even at the simpler end of the spectrum, some of today's mainstream web authoring tools include advanced visualization techniques. Looking at the maintenance of more structured content, perhaps based on fully-fledged ontologies, visualization becomes even more helpful.

The kind of technologies used for personalizing and recommending content to particular users based on their profiles may also turn out to be useful for knowledge assessment. For this purpose, one would construct artificial profiles not related to actual persons, but rather designed to specify the field of interest for assessment purposes. Finally, visualization techniques are a valuable help for the interpretation of the results of knowledge assessment.

Issues

Linking to further resources

One obvious way to add value to content through adaptation technologies is to always show links to further information on a topic together with the content currently displayed to the user. Further information, in this context, may be anything from relevant news items to elaborate eLearning courses. This would also address the lesson learned about the importance of promoting learning. However, it is not a standard feature of most systems today.

Adapting to intended use

Ideally, the way knowledge is presented should be perfectly adapted to the intended use of that knowledge. For systems expected to attempt such a feat, that means the intended use must be known to them. This poses a problem since the same content may be retrieved from a repository for very different kinds of use, so the content itself cannot serve as a guide in that matter.

There are technologies intended to make inferences about the current work context of a user, but unfortunately they are not very reliable yet. The issue thus becomes one of deciding, in the light of current technological capabilities, to what extent one wants to attempt automatically adapting content.

Identifying similar knowledge

Talking about intended uses is all very well, but what if available knowledge would be useful but is not in fact being used, because the knowledge worker concerned is not aware of it? One of the lessons learned has emphasized that steps should be taken to promote the use of available knowledge. Adaptation technologies can help by automatically displaying content in a way that encourages use as directly as possible, minimizing the effort users have to invest in adapting the content to their purposes themselves.

A consultant analyzing a situation, for instance, will usually find a list of pertinent questions more helpful than an academic treatise, even if the latter really contains the same knowledge. Automatically transforming one into the other, however, would require computers to actually understand the content, which is quite out of the question today. The issue, for the time being, is therefore to develop technology that can at least identify pieces of content containing the same meaning more accurately than possible so far. This will allow adaptation in the sense of selectively offering only the most appropriate of a number of items with similar content.

Such a selection presupposes that different adaptations of what is essentially the same content are already available in a repository. A related issue, therefore, is how to decide what kinds of knowledge should be stored in different adaptations, and what should be adapted on the fly by the system.

Adapting on the fly vs. in advance

Current technological limitations only narrow the range of what *can* be done; they do not tell one what *should* be done. Some kinds of content can be automatically adapted on the fly, but that may not always make sense. Conversely, some kinds of content require human intervention to be transformed into a different form, the cost of which may not be justified.

Another lesson learned has been that technology should always be under user control. In the context of adaptation technologies, this includes both questions of content, such as whether to show full texts or summaries of documents by default, and questions of layout, such as the preferred typeface and size.

Allowing individual customization

Obviously, this may conflict with some organizations' desire to maintain an appearance consistent with their corporate design in their intranet applications. One should keep in mind, however, that not offering customization options to users may result in lower productivity, both directly because of lower work efficiency and indirectly because of lower user satisfaction and motivation.

Finally, it is important to realize that the ideal to strive for is not always the perfect adaptation of the system to the current capabilities of the user. Instead, training the user to be able to use more sophisticated tools may be called for, which again highlights the lesson learned about the importance of developing knowledge skills.

Interpreting complex visualizations

For example, the most useful tool for a difficult job may well be a complex visualization that is far from easy to interpret. This invariably requires the user to learn how to understand that visualization. That learning effort may not be justified for casual users, but professional users will, in the long run, be better off with professional systems, even if they require some training.

Chapter 16

eLearning

Information technology has opened up a whole new range of possibilities for distance education. This chapter briefly describes the evolution of eLearning, outlines the most important components eLearning environments, assesses the relevance of eLearning to knowledge management, and identifies a number of open issues.

Overview

The first attempts to use computers for educational purposes went by the name of computer based training (CBT). Developed at a time when only few computers were networked, these were typically offline solutions distributed on floppy disks and later on CD-ROMs. Courses were delivered with the help of proprietary client software.

Computer based training

With the advent of the world wide web, delivering courses over the Internet became common. Instead of requiring specific client software, the web browser quickly established itself as the client of choice. Web based training (WBT) shifted the provision of course content to servers. At the same time, the first systems appeared which permitted learners to communicate with trainers as well as other learners.

Web based training

Basically, however, WBT was just CBT delivered through the web. The term eLearning, as it is used today, has a more general focus and encompasses a wide range of related aspects. Delivery, for instance, may by accomplished by just about any electronic medium, including the public world wide web, corporate intranets, and DVDs.

eLearning

Beyond technology issues, eLearning is also concerned with individual learning styles and instructional design, as well as with appropriate ways of employing eLearning. In particular, reaping the benefits of both traditional face-to-face instruction and eLearning by mixing them in a planned fashion is becoming ever more common.

More emphasis is now being placed on the content of courses. While in the early days of WBT the technology stood at the center of attention, the production of eLearning course content has meanwhile evolved into an industry of its own. Specialists design multimedia and interactive content. Furthermore, standards are emerging in order to permit the integration of content from third-party sources with custom content tailored to the specific requirements of the organization. More attention is now also being paid to the roles of learners and trainers, and how they ought to be managed.

All those aspects are addressed by comprehensive software solutions known as learning management systems. Environments supporting eLearning typically consist of components for authoring, content and user administration, course delivery, communication and collaboration, testing, and collecting feedback.

Authoring   Authoring in an eLearning context refers both to creating new content and to reusing existing modules. Specialized tools aiding individual authors in creating new courses from scratch have been around for quite some time. The focus is now on allowing multiple authors to collaboratively develop a course and on supporting the efficient reuse of available materials.

Administration   Easy administration of content on the one hand, and of learners and trainers on the other, is usually seen as an important feature, particularly as the provision of courses is increasingly being outsourced to external service providers. Tracking the progress of individual learners and of whole classes also falls under the heading of administration.

Delivery   The component delivering the course itself is the most critical one in terms of performance and scalability. An appropriate user interface has to be provided, including navigation facilities suitable for both the target group and the course content.

Communication   The course materials are not the only opportunity for learning in eLearning environments. A broad range of communication technologies such as email, discussion forums, instant messaging, chatrooms, and video conferencing are used to connect learners with each other and with trainers. Annotation facilities can serve the same purpose.

Testing comes in two flavors: First, people may take tests in order to find out which courses are suitable for them. Second, tests are of course being used to assess the extent to which course objectives have been achieved. Testing may be made both more efficient and less wearing for the learner through personalization. Testing

Finally, feedback on all aspects of the process from a user's perspective may be collected either actively, by asking the learners, or passively, by tracking and analyzing the usage of the system. Feedback

Relevance to Knowledge Management

One contribution of eLearning environments to knowledge management lies in the fact that they often constitute a cost-efficient way of transferring knowledge. While initial costs may be high because of the necessity to develop a new course tailored to a particular company, the costs associated with the subsequent deployment of that course can be very low.

This is really the knowledge economy's law of increasing returns in disguise: Rather than yielding more and more profits the wider a product is disseminated, this is about saving more and more costs. Large companies on tight budgets will therefore find eLearning highly relevant if their knowledge management efforts involve further education for many employees, particularly if those employees are geographically dispersed.

Perhaps even more importantly, however, eLearning can enable learning in situations in which it would otherwise not be possible at all, since it can be deployed to more employees more quickly than traditional trainer-led seminars. Bringing tens of thousands of employees up to date about a new product within a day, for example, will generally be impossible with traditional methods.

Furthermore, eLearning is a natural field of common interest of different departments like human resources and information technology. While this may sometimes give rise to conflict, it may also be an opportunity encouraging convergence, a kind of catalyst leading to a better understanding

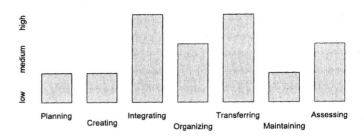

Figure 16.1. The contribution of eLearning technologies to the various knowledge management processes.

between those departments, which can only benefit the overall knowledge management effort.

Figure 16.1 shows the extent to which eLearning technologies support the various knowledge management processes.

Knowledge planning does not seem to benefit from eLearning in any particular fashion. Of course, some of the background knowledge required for making the necessary decisions might have been acquired through eLearning. In general, however, personal experience and familiarity with the business in question are more important here.

Since knowledge creation refers to the development of knowledge that is really new, as opposed to educating employees by offering them access to already existing knowledge that is only new to them personally, eLearning does not have much to contribute to this process.

By contrast, the attempt to make knowledge available to employees in an integrated fashion stands to gain a lot from eLearning. For one thing, eLearning courses may be developed based on the expertise of employees, thereby making much of their knowledge available to the company at large.

Template-based authoring tools that are particularly easy to use and incorporate instructional design principles have been developed for the design of eLearning courses. With such tools, more of the employees' knowledge is likely to be explicated and made available to others on a broad basis. Furthermore, opportunities to systematically build up relevant knowledge may quickly and easily be made available to employees by licensing existing courses offered by external eLearning content providers.

Developing an eLearning course inevitably means that in-

dividual pieces of knowledge have to be arranged in a coherent manner. At the very least, content will be presented
in a sequence that makes sense to the learner, and a table of
contents will be provided. Ideally, there will be many different paths through the course material along which learners
can be guided based on their particular prior knowledge and
personal learning styles. Additional features like glossaries
linked to relevant parts of the course may also be provided.

Organizing

All these structural elements of eLearning courses may
either be reused in some form in a larger corporate knowledge
repository, or they may in fact be based on the way such a
repository is organized. Either way, having similar structural
elements in eLearning courses and a corporate repository will
enhance the latter's usefulness as a background library to the
former.

Knowledge transfer is of course the very reason of existence for eLearning environments. But it is not only the
knowledge contained in the courses that is transferred with
the help of eLearning systems. Rather, the communication
facilities offered by most eLearning environments will often also be used for transferring additional knowledge when
teachers and tutors answer students' questions. Through the
same facilities, students may also engage in informal knowledge transfer among each other.

Transferring

On a more abstract level, eLearning may be regarded as
an addition to the list of possible channels for knowledge
transfer, making it easier for different people with different
learning styles to chose a channel appropriate to their personal needs and preferences.

There are no particular benefits that eLearning brings for
the maintenance of knowledge. The current generation of
eLearning course authoring tools is still more suited to producing new courses than to maintain existing content in a
really flexible way.

Maintaining

Tests as a means to verify whether the knowledge offered
in eLearning courses has been successfully absorbed by the
learner are important to knowledge assessing efforts with a
more general focus in two ways.

Assessing

First, the data gained this way may of course be used in
constructing intellectual capital statements. In fact, this applies not only to data from tests at the end of a course or unit,
but also to tests which are conducted beforehand in order to

select appropriate courses. Combined, the results from these two kinds of tests provide a picture that covers not only of the current level of knowledge of employees, but also of the extent to which eLearning has helped in closing knowledge gaps.

The second way in which tests are important for more general knowledge assessment is through their ubiquity in all kinds of eLearning courses. Assessment is an accepted part of eLearning and is being taken for granted. This stands in stark contrast to other knowledge management efforts, where very often no culture of measurement exists. Experience with eLearning may therefore help to establish knowledge assessment as an accepted part of knowledge management as a whole.

Issues

Appropriate use of eLearning

First, it should be noted that for all its benefits, eLearning must not be regarded as a panacea. Some aspects of traditional classroom teaching are difficult if not impossible to replicate in an online setting. Also, eLearning will never be able to convey the kind of tacit knowledge one develops in the course of an apprenticeship. Even when it comes to teaching explicit knowledge, empirical evidence suggests that the appropriateness of eLearning also depends on the individual learning styles of the students concerned [103].

In the end, the decision on whether eLearning is appropriate or not will have to be made on a case-to-case basis, weighing the perceived benefits against the aspects of traditional methods of learning that eLearning is unable to provide. The aim is blended learning, finding the right mix of different methods.

Adaptation to the target audience

In traditional seminars, it is fairly easy for a skilled teacher to adapt both the content and the style of delivery to the needs of the audience. To achieve a similar level of adaptivity through eLearning systems, by contrast, is a big challenge for software developers and course authors alike.

The problem lies not only in the process of adaptation itself, but also in gathering the feedback necessary to decide on appropriate changes. A teacher in a seminar will use lots nonverbal cues from the audience for this purpose, which are not available to eLearning software. Thus a thorough understanding of the target audience in advance is even more important for authoring eLearning courses than it is for preparing traditional teaching sessions.

In theory, eLearning offers the opportunity for tailoring the curriculum not only to a target audience the size of a typical seminar group, but to a target audience of one: Completely individualized learning. In practice, further research is needed in order to be able to seize that opportunity.

The lesson learned in chapter 3 about the importance of promoting the actual use of knowledge can be addressed by eLearning through appropriate course design. Textbooks usually do not consist of theory only; rather, they include examples which not only aid understanding, but also engage the minds of the readers in a way that makes it more likely for them to remember the content later when it is needed. *Use of multimedia and interactivity*

In eLearning environments, course authors can achieve the same effect even more effectively: Multimedia and interactive elements like simulations go far beyond what is possible in textbooks. Unlike textbooks, eLearning environments can support the form of learning that is arguably the most important one: Learning by doing [141]. However, there is not nearly as much experience with course design for eLearning systems as there is with writing textbooks. Getting the balances right and using the new possibilities in really sensible ways rather than just eye-catching ones is not yet a matter of course today.

As one lesson learned has pointed out, new technologies should integrate existing systems and content. In the context of eLearning, the obvious way to do this, apart from including existing resources when authoring courses, is to also provide links to knowledge outside the eLearning environment for students who want to know more about a topic than is covered in the course. *Integration of existing resources*

Corporate repositories, subscribed information services, and the public Internet may thus act as a huge background library for the eLearning environment. What is still not clear, however, is how to best approach this task and precisely how much the effort going into establishing such links is warranted by actual benefits for students.

Addressing the lesson learned that technology should always be under user control can mean two things for eLearning systems. First, there is the obvious fact that knowledge delivered through eLearning allows the user more control over the *User control* process. One just cannot hit a "pause"-button in the middle of a traditional classroom lecture. On the other hand, complete freedom will not lead to the most efficient way of learning either. That is hardly a new realization, but discoveries long established in fields like psychology and educational science have not always found their way into the design of eLearning systems yet.

The second and more controversial issue is how to deal with the competency and interest profiles that systems build and maintain. Users may be concerned about privacy issues, while companies may want to exploit such profiles also for knowledge management purposes beyond eLearning.

Influence on culture

One of the most important lessons learned has been emphasizing the central role of organizational culture for knowledge management. In the context of eLearning, this raises an interesting question: To what extent can eLearning convey not just facts, but also help with developing or reinforcing an appropriate culture?

Since even reading a well-written book can change one's perspective on many matters, it stands to reason that eLearning courses incorporating interactive elements and tailored specifically to a particular company may prove even more useful for that purpose. There has, however, been little research so far systematically examining this issue.

Trust

A particularly significant success factor for eLearning is the trust that learners place in the content, in the teachers, and in the system itself. The lesson learned about promoting trust applies to eLearning with a special emphasis on electronically mediated relationships between learners and teachers.

While technology cannot, of course, be a solution in itself, some eLearning environments have already been designed with this issue in mind [167]. On the whole, however, more research is needed on ways in which technology can help foster trust.

Incentives

Among the more controversial aspects of knowledge management highlighted by the lessons learned have been incentive and reward systems. Depending on the motivation of employees to participate in eLearning programs, incentives may be necessary to get them to participate at all. If, on the other hand, motivation is generally high, then the opportunity to participate in an eLearning program may in itself be a reward for other things. The key here obviously lies in employees' motivation, which may be very hard to assess reliably.

For human resources managers, skills management is an important topic, for instance with a view to succession planning. This is an area where eLearning systems could make a significant contribution: The user profiles they employ in order to tailor both the course content and its presentation to the learner could either be used in a more general skills management setting, or they might in fact be drawn from a skills management system in the first place. Today, however, eLearning environments and skills management systems are generally not yet integrated to the extent required for such seamless interoperation.

Skills management

Finally, there has been the lesson learned to also take the built environment into consideration. Applied to eLearning, this raises the issue of where the learning is supposed to take place. Whether this will be in an open-plan office, one's own office, a dedicated room at the workplace, or at home, will have consequences concerning the efficiency that can be expected from eLearning.

Where and when to learn

Technical considerations need to be taken into account as well: While bandwidth may not be an issue at work any more, some employees may still be using slow dial-up lines at home. All this is closely tied to when employees are supposed to learn. If management, for instance, considers eLearning to be secondary to everything else, to be performed at the workplace, between other tasks, when time permits, then exciting results can hardly be expected.

Chapter 17

Personal Tools

Knowledge management solutions developed with organizational goals in mind often tend to neglect the perspective of the individual user. Personal knowledge tools, by contrast, focus primarily on the needs of the individual. Although some of these tools do have features for collaborating and sharing knowledge with other people, their most important aim is to support knowledge management in a way that accommodates individual thinking styles and working habits.

This chapter first provides an overview of such tools, starting with special-purpose applications and moving on to tools integrating several applications. After that, their relevance to knowledge management is discussed and open issues are pointed out.

Overview

Taking notes and organizing them is only inadequately supported by most text editing software. Outliners are better suited for that purpose. They allow people to easily arrange and rearrange their notes in a hierarchical fashion. Even more flexible are concept mapping applications, which do not limit the structure to a hierarchy.

Note taking and organizing

Specialized tools make it easy to capture snippets of information from different sources like web pages, local files, and emails. Snippets can consist of both text and multimedia elements, and copies of all of them are stored in a personal repository along with a reference to their original location.

Capturing

Such personal repositories can then be browsed chrono-

Retrieving

logically. Snippets can also be retrieved by full-text searching. Personal retrieval tools of another kind focus not just on snippets deliberately captured by the user, but rather index the whole hard disk, providing powerful full-text search capabilities for local files, including many proprietary formats. The access to Internet search engines can also be personalized through appropriate tools.

Diaries

Electronic diaries can also make personal knowledge management easier. The term refers not just to people's notes on their activities, but also to systems automatically keeping track of things like email and phone contacts, documents and applications used, and web sites visited. The human mind tends to think contextually and chronologically. An electronic diary is often the most efficient method of quickly locating content or contacts based on memories of past events.

Bookmark management

Many people have bookmark collections pointing to thousands of websites. Most web browsers come with a bookmark management component supporting a hierarchical structure. However, specialized tools offer more flexibility and functionality, including independence from a particular browser, better search and maintenance features, and automatic categorization.

Personal databases

Bookmarks are of course not the only kind of information chunks that are usually handled by small databases. Apart from tools like address books, which are common to all businesses, personal databases also include more specialized applications such as bibliography management in research settings.

Integrated tools

The tools discussed so far in this chapter focus on parts of personal knowledge management, but do certainly not cover all of it. Attempts to offer integrated support for knowledge management at the personal level are unfortunately even scarcer.

There are, however, a few applications drawing synergies from the combination of several of the applications mentioned above. Retrieval of local files, for instance, benefits from using typical personal information like contacts and schedules in order to determine the context of files and make them accessible in a more useful way.

Working alongside web browsers, tools can also blur the boundary between bookmarks and browsing histories [31]. This is especially interesting because the analysis of surfing patterns may reveal more useful categories than the folder structure users themselves create for storing their bookmarks.

Some of the tools developed for assisting professional researchers constitute the most ambitious attempts at integration. They combine elements of capturing, organizing, and retrieving with the management of both bookmarks and bibliographies.

Relevance to Knowledge Management

A number of the lessons learned in chapter 3 show the practical importance of personal knowledge tools. The very first one has been that knowledge management is primarily about people. This does not only mean groups of people. It also implies that the needs of individuals have to be given due consideration. These individual needs also have to be supported by appropriate technology.

The lessons learned have also pointed out the importance of individual motivation in general, and of obtaining buy-in for knowledge management projects in particular. Both of these lessons learned are addressed by personal knowledge tools, since a positive answer to the question "What's in it for me?" is much easier for employees when talking about tools directly addressing their needs. Offering personal knowledge tools to employees is therefore a very good way of obtaining buy-in and sustaining motivation.

The need to emphasize learning and integrate knowledge management with training have also been among the lessons learned. Now this does not only mean sitting through seminars. It also means taking notes there, reviewing those notes later, finding connections to other personal knowledge and integrating the new with the old. These are tasks at which personal knowledge tools excel. No other kind of technology offers better support for these aspects of learning.

Another lesson learned has emphasized promoting collaboration. At first glance, this may appear not to be one of the strong areas of personal knowledge tools. Indeed, they often do not directly support collaboration in a particularly useful manner. They may, however, be very valuable in creating the preconditions for successful collaboration.

Consider, for example, the case of a meeting aimed at knowledge creation. Such meetings stand to benefit a lot from the explication of the different mental models of the

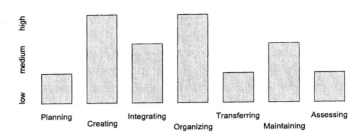

Figure 17.1. The contribution of personal tools to the various knowledge management processes.

participants [135]. If everybody were to bring a detailed concept map of their view of the topic into the meeting, that would considerably increase the quality of the meeting.

Normally, however, few people will take the time and effort required to explicate their mental models by preparing such a concept map just for this one meeting. If, on the other hand, they are working with personal knowledge tools on a daily basis, chances are that many of them will already have such concept maps, which they originally created for their own purposes. Now they just need to bring them along rather than create them under time pressure. So indirectly, the availability of personal knowledge tools leads to increased explication and sharing of mental models and thereby to enhanced quality of collaboration.

Figure 17.1 shows the extent to which personal tools support the various knowledge management processes.

Planning, as usual, does not benefit a lot from technology. This applies to tools with a personal focus in much the same manner as it does to other tools.

Knowledge creation, by contrast, can be expected to derive major benefits from personal knowledge tools. On the one hand, creative thinking is aided by subjecting oneself to new and different perspectives and adapting and expanding one's own mental models accordingly. On the other hand, dealing with complex issues in an effective and efficient manner often benefits from tools aiding the structuring of thoughts and from visual feedback when playing around with those thoughts. Personal knowledge tools like concept mapping applications provide this kind of assistance.

Even disregarding that dynamic component for a moment and considering only the presentation of prior knowledge in a form conducive to creative thinking, personal knowledge tools still seem to be the most promising solution. This is because they present content in a way which is based on the individual mental models of the user rather than in the one-size-fits-all fashion typical for content drawn from outside sources like corporate repositories, commercial databases, or the Internet. The kind of personalization technologies discussed in chapter 15 can alleviate this problem, but will never attain the level of truly personal knowledge tools.

How are notes being taken today? Usually on sketchpads, flipcharts, whiteboards, or perhaps with a word processor. Personal knowledge tools offer a more satisfactory solution. For one thing, they increase employee satisfaction because people can have it "their way". More importantly with re-gard to knowledge integration, without appropriate personal knowledge tools, people will typically resort to using paper when they want to avoid the restrictions of standard office applications like word processors. Therefore, notes will not be available electronically at all in many cases unless suitable personal knowledge tools are being offered.

Integrating

Knowledge integration at the enterprise level also bene-fits in an indirect fashion. Corporate repositories will often attract more content if employees are using personal knowl-edge tools. The reason for this is that such tools encourage the explication of knowledge. It is psychologically easier for people to let others have a look at knowledge that they have already explicated for their own purposes than to take the time to sit down share their knowledge without obvious benefit to them.

Beyond just taking notes by jotting down items as they occur, there is the question of how to organize them. Letting employees organize knowledge for their personal purposes with the help of more appropriate tools is likely to lead to better results in two ways.

Organizing

First, just as with knowledge integration, there is a ben-efit at the enterprise level: The knowledge will not only be available electronically, but will typically also come in a more structured form than notes typed into a text editor. That struc-ture may be used for organizing knowledge at the enterprise level as well, either directly by mapping it onto other structures, or indirectly by using it to identify relevant metadata more easily.

Second, organizing knowledge with the help of appropriate personal knowledge tools will not only make that knowledge available digitally, but also increase the efficiency of the knowledge worker at future tasks involving that knowledge; after all, he now has it at his fingertips in a way that precisely fits his own mental model.

The very same reasons that make personal knowledge tools the perfect choice for integrating and organizing knowledge unfortunately limit their use for transferring knowledge. Being perfectly adapted to one person's mental model makes content harder to understand for others. Besides, in terms of actually available products in this segment, while some do also offer collaboration functionalities that could be used to aid knowledge transfer, this tends not to be their strong side.

Maintaining

Maintaining knowledge is, of course, easier for people if it resides in personal knowledge tools or can at least be accessed and manipulated through them. Perhaps even more important, however, is the fact that people tend to develop a sense of ownership for knowledge that they originally captured with their personal knowledge tools. They are therefore more likely to keep such knowledge up to date.

Assessing

In most cases, personal knowledge tools cannot make much of a contribution to knowledge assessment. They may be able to provide data like the number of bookmarks or bibliographic records per employee, but these will rarely be particularly useful indicators.

Issues

Conflicting requirements

The company as a whole and the individual knowledge workers have different, and sometimes conflicting, requirements. The lessons learned have shown that a number of balances need to be struck in knowledge management. The balance between an organizational and an individual focus should be added to that list.

This issue has so far not received nearly as much attention as it deserves, neither in theory nor in practice. Even in the academic literature, little can be found about personal knowledge management in general, let alone the design of suitable tools and their relationship to enterprise-wide solutions.

In practice, while there is much talk about personalization, available products rarely can be said to truly support personal knowledge management. Those that come close typically are not systems with an organizational focus and personalization components, but rather the kind of personal knowledge tools described in this chapter, most of which do not support organizational knowledge management to the extent that would be desirable. In other words, there is a lack of integration between tools with a personal focus and systems with an organizational focus.

Need for integrated solutions

Ease of use is particularly important for knowledge management tools, as one of the lessons learned has pointed out. Unfortunately, personal knowledge tools, especially some of the more innovative ones, and those aimed at supporting knowledge creation in particular, have a tendency towards non-standard user interfaces and the use of metaphors unfamiliar to many people.

Non-standard user interfaces

That is not to say that all personal knowledge tools should strictly adhere to established standards. Indeed, this would often be impossible precisely because of the innovative nature of such tools. For example, using the concept of zooming for navigation in a typically loosely structured personal collection of ideas may significantly increase the user's overview compared to traditional methods like collapsible outlines. However, tools deliberately breaking with user interface standards are often perceived as "unprofessional" in the business community.

This issue can only be addressed by increased efforts on both sides: Developers have to take more care to break with standards only when really necessary, and advocates of a tool in a company need to educate their peers about its benefits. The latter is another example of the lesson learned about the importance of internal marketing for knowledge management technologies.

Chapter 18

Artificial Intelligence

Artificial intelligence research has been dealing with knowledge in computer systems long before knowledge management became a popular concept in business. This chapter provides a brief overview of some important artificial intelligence technologies, assesses their relevance to knowledge management, and points out issues arising in this context.

Overview

A fundamental prerequisite for many artificial intelligence methods are suitable ways of representing knowledge. Automated reasoning typically uses highly formalized knowledge bases consisting of explicit rules, using for example modal logic, predicate logic, or temporal logic. People, on the other hand, often find it easier to work with object-oriented forms of knowledge representation, which for instance permit sub-objects to inherit properties from their parents. A third type of knowledge representation is based on graphs, for example semantic networks.

Knowledge representation

Many common forms of knowledge representations are really just different ways of expressing the same things, but optimized for different tasks. Accordingly, knowledge is frequently converted from one form of representation to another, depending on what the knowledge in question will be used for.

Expert systems use an inference engine to draw conclusions from a knowledge base. Fuzzy logic may be used in order to deal with ambiguity by not considering a given propo-

Expert systems and fuzzy logic

sition to be either true or false, but instead also allowing a range of values in between.

A typical application of an expert system would be to aid physicians in diagnosing diseases based on the symptoms observed in given case and the system's knowledge base containing the field's state of the art. In business settings, expert systems are frequently employed as decision support systems as well. By specifying and weighting different sets of criteria, one can use such systems to track the influences of various parameters.

Natural language processing   Natural language leaves much unstated and the meaning of statements often depends on their context. Linguistic technologies deal with automated parsing and understanding of texts as well as related endeavors such as automated translation. Furthermore, natural language processing is also concerned with speech recognition and synthesis.

Document analysis   Document analysis technologies cover a wide range of tasks from automatically determining the language and the genre of a given document to discovering relationships between documents in large repositories. Specialized methods deal with extracting data from unstructured documents of a known type.

Summarization   A particularly important part of document analysis is summarization. One way to achieve this is to identify the most relevant portions of a document and use the resulting extract as a summary. A more ambitious goal for summarizing texts is to automatically produce a more readable abstract consisting not just of parts of the original text, but also of text created by the system itself. Multi-document summarization deals with collections of related documents. Summarization may be generic in the sense that it is based only on document content, or it may produce summaries specifically tailored to a particular user or group.

Machine learning   Artificial intelligence also includes methods that let systems themselves enhance the knowledge they already embody. Inductive learning works by feeding the system with training examples consisting of inputs as well as the corresponding desired outputs. In this kind of supervised learning, the system analyzes correlations between those inputs and outputs and then adjusts itself in order to produce the desired kind of output in the future not only for the training inputs, but also for different but similar ones.

Artificial neural networks are a well-known technology employing this approach. They consist of large numbers of nodes connected by weighted links and they learn by adjusting those weights through repetitive learning cycles. Neural networks are particularly good at tasks like pattern recognition.

Another approach to machine learning consists of not trying to immediately generalize experiences, but rather store them as they are and adapt their lessons when needed. This is called instance-based learning and is exemplified by case based reasoning systems.

Methods of artificial intelligence are particularly useful for categorizing pieces of content, be they short email messages, longer text documents, or images. Segmentation is the task of finding a suitable set of categories for a given collection of objects. Clustering methods help to automate segmentation. Classification is the task of assigning objects to predefined categories. Both segmentation and classification are supported by specialized variants of artificial intelligence methods, particularly by natural language processing and machine learning.

Segmentation and classification

Intelligent agents are pieces of software capable of acting autonomously on their user's behalf. They perceive their environment, evaluate choices in the light of goals, and can decide on actions without checking back with the user. A typical application would be an agent regularly gathering information on a certain topic and alerting its owner to the most important discoveries.

Intelligent agents

Multi-agent systems allow different agents to interact with each other, for instance by sharing information or by copying another agent's behavior. This way, agent technology can be used for applications such as automated negotiations.

Relevance to Knowledge Management

Some of the work done in the domain of knowledge engineering, the term associated with many of the methods originating in artificial intelligence research, is currently being rebranded as knowledge management. Let us therefore get one thing straight before proceeding. Most knowledge management efforts do not use artificial intelligence techniques, nor do they need to. When knowledge engineering methods are being promoted as an absolutely necessary cornerstone of knowledge management, this is often a case of trying to protect past investments of time and effort—the scientific community's equivalent to technology vendors sticking the label knowledge management onto their old database software in order to benefit from the current hype.

Having said that, however, there are many areas of knowledge management where artificial intelligence technologies can indeed make a most welcome contribution. For example, one of the lessons learned in chapter 3 has pointed out the importance of not just collecting knowledge, but also promoting its reuse. Technologies making relevant content more likely to be found within the time constraints of everyday work help to achieve that aim. Automated summarization of documents is one such technology. Another lesson learned has been to connect people to information in new ways. Intelligent agents can help with that, as can document analysis technologies which infer connections between documents and people.

The importance of ease of use has also been emphasized by the lessons learned. Artificial intelligence technologies like agents may contribute to the usability of other tools. In fact, an example based on the lesson learned to embed knowledge management in work processes seems to almost demand the power of artificial intelligence: If a system is to proactively suggest relevant content based on the user's current work context, the issue of guessing when the system should or should not interrupt the user may only be solved adequately by employing methods of artificial intelligence. On a more general level, it may be argued that in the long term, artificial intelligence is our best chance to develop technology adapting itself to people, rather than requiring people to change their ways because of technological limitations.

Perhaps one of the most elusive goals sometimes pursued in knowledge management is the attempt to have systems capture tacit knowledge. Neural networks may, indeed, achieve this up to a point. They do not require explicit rules, but can learn from examples provided by human experts who act on tacit knowledge and who would not, if asked to, be able to formulate such explicit rules.

Figure 18.1 shows the extent to which artificial intelligence technologies support the various knowledge management processes.

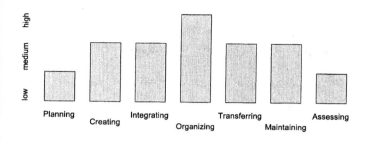

Figure 18.1. The contribution of artificial intelligence to the various knowledge management processes.

Technology in general does not have much to offer in support of planning for knowledge management. This also applies to artificial intelligence technologies.

Knowledge creation is primarily the domain of people, not of machines. Nevertheless, it can be argued that some of the technologies embraced by the term artificial intelligence are in fact capable of adding value to information in a way that transforms that information into something closer to what one might call knowledge. Artificial intelligence methods employed in document analysis and automated classification can be regarded as means to place documents in a context in an automated fashion. In a similar vein, clustering can be used for category generation to identify contexts which may not have been apparent to human editors.

A massive body of both theory and practical experience with formal knowledge representation has grown out of artificial intelligence research over the past few decades. Dealing with knowledge at this very structured level marks the top end of knowledge integration efforts. Ideally, one would have all explicit knowledge available in such a formalized form. In practice, the task of knowledge integration is to make knowledge available on a broad basis at reasonable cost. Artificial intelligence not only sets the standards to aspire to in terms of knowledge representation, but through technologies like intelligent agents also provides tools which help to identify material worth integrating into a corporate repository from outside sources.

The process of organizing knowledge stands to gain even more from artificial intelligence, since this is where clustering and automated classification come into their own. They help both with creating structures appropriate to a given collection of documents and with adding new documents to those structures later on. Intelligent document analysis techniques may also go a long way towards automating the assignment of metadata to content.

Transferring

Intelligent agents not only support knowledge integration by identifying content worth integrating into a corporate repository from outside sources. They also support knowledge transfer by identifying content worth transferring to employees from a corporate repository. In that case, it is the software agent who alerts the user. If, on the other hand, knowledge transfer from a repository is being initiated by an employee through a search query, artificial intelligence technologies may also help: Natural language processing may be useful here.

Maintaining

The ways in which methods originating in artificial intelligence research support maintaining knowledge are similar to those in which they support organizing knowledge. Clustering and classification technologies are of course not limited to the initial structuring of a repository. Rather, they will typically be used on a continuous basis. If, for instance, lots of documents are added to a particular category, the clustering tool may respond by suggesting to split that category up into certain subcategories. Turning from the maintenance of the structure of a repository to the maintenance of the content itself, automated summarization can assist maintainers by reducing the time they need to judge whether content is still up to date and relevant.

Assessing

Knowledge assessment is unlikely to benefit much from artificial intelligence technologies. At most, automatic document summarization may help people charged with knowledge assessment a little by taking some work out of gaining an overview of what kinds of knowledge are available in explicit form.

Issues

Big upfront investments

The advice of the lesson learned to start small may be difficult to heed when it comes to some of the technologies discussed in this chapter. Automated classification of documents, for example, requires significant upfront investments and makes little sense for small volumes of content. And it is not just a question of quantity either. Expert systems, regardless of their size, require well-formalized knowledge bases. Putting these together usually requires highly qualified knowledge engineering specialists. Unlike with, for instance, repositories of essentially unstructured documents, not all employees can be regarded as potential contributors here.

A related issue is brought into focus by the lesson learned about understanding the real knowledge requirements of an organization. Artificial intelligence approaches often derive their power from the fact that knowledge is not only stored and made accessible to users, but that these systems are actually capable of reasoning. They are able to draw conclusions from the knowledge available to them. The issue here is whether the reasoning behind those conclusions needs to be explained to the user. If this is a requirement, that will rule out black-box approaches like neural networks in favor of the kind of symbolic inference found in classical expert systems.

Explaining automated reasoning

Natural language processing is likely to have a major impact on knowledge management capabilities in the future. It is already being used for judging the similarity not only of long text documents, but also of short questions posed by users of a system [25, 72]. This enables the system to respond by providing the answers given to similar questions in the past, rather than always having to consult human experts.

Identifying similarities and relationships

Artificial intelligence technologies become even more interesting when one looks beyond similarities of two documents. If document A is related to document B in some way, and B to C, than A and C are also somehow related. Finding measures for identifying relationships that do not lose their meaning through several such iterations seems a most promising field of research.

One final word of warning. The promises of artificial intelligence technologies can sound very tempting in the context of knowledge management. It is therefore important to keep in mind the lessons learned that technologies have to address real needs, and that technology is always a matter of pragmatism. The issue here is to also recognize the limitations of artificial intelligence technologies, both in terms of their current power and in terms of their applicability to a given problem. In many cases, something simpler than an artificial intelligence solution will do the job with a better cost/benefit ratio.

Recognizing limitations

Chapter 19

Networking

While people networks are central to knowledge management, computer networks do not play quite as prominent a role. They do, however, constitute an essential enabler of many knowledge management applications. This chapter provides a quick overview of network-related technologies one should be aware of, assesses their relevance to knowledge management, and discusses issues arising in connection with their use.

Overview

The term intranet is occasionally associated with particular applications, for instance file sharing, but what it really means is an organization's internal network that is based on standard Internet technologies rather than proprietary ones. Intranets are usually connected to the public Internet through a gateway. If that connection is used to open up part of the internal network to external parties, such as customers or suppliers, then that is an extranet.

Intranets and extranets

Unlike private networks based entirely on dedicated leased lines and kept physically separate from the Internet, extranets exchange data between different business locations over the public Internet. These communications are protected from prying eyes through authentication and encryption technologies: A virtual private network is established.

The usefulness of a network generally increases with its size. The larger a network grows, however, the more difficult it becomes to locate elements within it. Directory services

Directory services

like LDAP (Lightweight Directory Access Protocol), which can be distributed over several servers, allow searches for persons, organizations, organizational units, devices, and other resources. Most importantly, such a service drastically reduces the effort required to maintain that kind of information. Rather than having their own directories which would need to be administrated separately, all other applications requiring such information simply query this one central service.

Email   The most widespread network application is email. The email client software usually receives messages from a server in one of two ways. POP3 (Post Office Protocol 3) can only be used for a store and forward procedure: Messages are simply moved from the server to the client. IMAP (Internet Message Access Protocol), by contrast, also allows messages to remain on the server where they can be managed remotely. For sending email, SMTP (Simple Mail Transfer Protocol) is the dominant technology.

A close second behind email, the web is a network application designed for real-time interaction. Both the public world wide web and intranet websites today often incorporate elements dynamically generated for each request. Whole software applications have been made accessible through the web, relying on a broad range of technologies.

Web servers   On the server side, dynamic websites are usually achieved through servlets, little pieces of code executed by the server on demand. For simple applications, these might be script written in a programming language like Perl or Python and accessed through CGI (Common Gateway Interface). PHP is a popular scripting language for code embedded in web pages and executed by the server just before transmitting those pages. More ambitious projects will typically use a separate application server. Java is the programming language of choice here. Such servlets can be invoked through JSP (Java Server Pages).

Web browsers   On the client side, web browsers interpret different kinds of instructions which are collectively referred to as DHTML (Dynamic Hypertext Markup Language). Again, for demanding applications Java is frequently employed as a programming language. Such pieces of code, executed locally on the client machine, are called applets.

Web browsers also manage Cookies, little pieces of data stored on the client machine by websites and retrieved at sub-

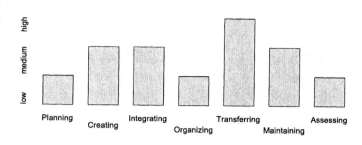

Figure 19.1. The contribution of networking technologies to the various knowledge management processes.

sequent visits to the respective website. This technology is primarily used for keeping track of individual users and their preferences. If the data exchanged between web browsers and servers is to be encrypted, this is usually accomplished through SSL (Secure Sockets Layer) or its successor, TLS (Transport Layer Security).

Relevance to Knowledge Management

While the role of network technologies may be nothing more than the provision of an appropriate infrastructure for a number of knowledge management applications, it is important to realize how essential that infrastructure is for many purposes. If an employee's personal computer is down for some reason, this may be a major nuisance, but a company should be able to overcome that problem fairly quickly. By contrast, if there is a problem with the external network connection, there may be little the company can do about it. Since communicating with the outside world is an important part of knowledge management, this highlights the relevance of reliable network technologies.

Figure 19.1 shows the extent to which networking technologies support the various knowledge management processes.

Knowledge planning usually involves mainly face-to-face communication. Network technologies thus do not have a significant impact on that process.

While the most effective knowledge creation activities probably also take place in face-to-face settings, there are some areas where network technologies can make a contribution. On the one hand, network technologies underpin all

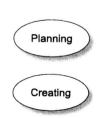

virtual collaborative activities like large-scale asynchronous brainstorming. This is the infrastructure function of network technologies.

On the other hand, today's technologies for transmitting and rendering rich and dynamic content permit users to access online applications via their standard web browsers. This may enable or encourage a much larger number of people to participate in knowledge creation activities, which will often lead to superior results in terms of both quantity and quality. Network technologies also have a positive impact on knowledge creation activities because they are often necessary in order to access existing knowledge, check hypotheses, and get stimuli for new ideas.

Integrating

Network technologies are relevant to knowledge integration because knowledge that is being captured electronically today usually finds its way to a repository from some other source on the network. This applies not only to the intranet in an office setting. An extranet may be the prerequisite for obtaining valuable knowledge from customers, suppliers, and partners. Mobile members of the workforce such as salespeople may contribute knowledge for integration into a central repository on the spot through wireless data connections. Finally, many services providing content tailored specifically to the needs of particular companies deliver that content via the Internet.

Overall, the importance of network technologies for integrating knowledge is therefore considerable. In spite of that, however, these technologies do not merit maximum marks since they cannot really help a lot with the crucial people-oriented aspects of knowledge integration, such as recruiting the right people.

Organizing

Organizing knowledge is primarily about managing the structure of available knowledge. While some activities like manually classifying items of knowledge in a repository are typically performed remotely over the network, they are not inherently dependent on network technologies and could also be accomplished locally. Network technologies thus are not particularly relevant to organizing knowledge.

Transferring

Knowledge transfer is of course frequently being conducted via networks. Technologies ranging from simple intranets to virtual private networks including wireless access are a prerequisite for electronically transferring knowledge from person to person, between persons and repositories, and between different systems.

Maintaining knowledge benefits from network technologies to a certain extent because tasks like automatically updating content residing on remote servers require such technologies. The delivery of alerts about content having reached its expiry date also requires networks. The role of network technologies for knowledge maintenance is thus that of a handy helper, but not necessarily that of a sine qua non.

Assessing knowledge will rarely rely on network technologies to any great extent. Values for most of the indicators used for this purpose are usually assigned by people and not being reported constantly, but rather in periodic intervals, for instance quarterly. Network technologies therefore have little to offer in support of this process.

Issues

Most knowledge management applications can be implemented on the basis of a variety of different network technologies. Dynamic components of an intranet site, for example, may use DHTML or Java applets on the client side. On the server side, CGI scripts or Java servlets may do the job. In order to be able to choose appropriate technologies, one will of course have to estimate the bandwidth and response time demands of the application in question. Will there, for instance, be live video streaming?

Choosing technologies

Beyond that, likely future developments also have to be considered. Scalability and maintainability are key issues here. This is really just one of the lesson learned in chapter 3 in a new guise: Understand the knowledge requirements, here with a special emphasis on planning for the future.

Newer protocols may have many advantages, but they will sometimes not be understood by available software. Take email as a simple example. IMAP with its server-side storage and subscription features will probably be a more natural choice for most knowledge management efforts than POP3. However, a number of popular email clients support only POP3. Forcing an entire company to switch to a new email client may not be warranted. There are, of course, tools that make IMAP servers accessible via POP3, but most of the benefits of the more advanced protocol usually get lost on the way.

Old protocols

Security   The reason why knowledge management became so popular is of course that knowledge is such a valuable resource.
Security issues related to network technologies employed for
knowledge management purposes therefore are a natural area
of concern. This refers not only to the obvious need of system administration staff to patch security holes in software
as soon as possible, but also to senior management deciding
what level of protection is needed for what kind of content.
Technical solutions can range from the transparent encryption of virtual private networks to surveillance countermea-
sures like electromagnetic shielding.

Chapter 20

Standards

No single software package can serve all knowledge management purposes. Trying to standardize the functionality of systems may not make much sense, but appropriate standards for exchanging information will allow different tools to work together. This chapter surveys the most important standards, discusses their relevance to knowledge management, and points out issues to be considered in this context.

Overview

Many books have been published on most of the standards mentioned in this chapter. The aim here is not to explain these standards in detail, but rather to provide an overview of names and concepts of which one should be aware in the context of knowledge management.

Many text documents are still being kept in the proprietary **Text** formats of specific word processors. A few of those formats have become de facto standards and are understood by many third-party applications. Some text file formats, for instance RTF (Rich Text Format), have been deliberately designed for the purpose of exchanging texts between different word processors and operating systems.

Markup consists of special command sequences, often called tags, in a text file which indicate the logical structure of the document (for instance by distinguishing headlines) or formatting instructions (for example by specifying typefaces). The best known markup language is HTML (Hypertext Markup Language), the standard employed for web pages. SGML (Standard Generalized Markup Language) is not in itself a language for writing text documents but rather a standard for creating different kinds of markup languages. XML (Extensible Markup Language) is a simpler version of SGML and is now the standard of choice for most applications.

Structure Some standards have been devised specifically for encoding the kind of structures typically used to organize knowledge. OPML (Outline Processor Markup Language), an XML-based format, handles hierarchical structures. The Topic Maps standard goes beyond that by allowing arbitrary relationships between typed nodes. XTM (XML Topic Maps) is a standard for encoding Topic Maps based on XML.

Apart from these standards dealing with how to encode structure, a number of standards specify the content of particular structures for organizing knowledge. Most prominent among them are the classification schemes libraries employ to organize their collections. The most widely used one is the DDC (Dewey Decimal Classification). The UDC (Universal Decimal Classification) is an expansion of the DDC. The LCC (Library of Congress Classification) has also been adopted by many organizations around the world.

Other schemes cater to more specific needs, such as the ACM CCS (Association for Computing Machinery's Computing Classification System). More recently, classification schemes have been developed specifically for Internet resources. Of those, the ODP (Open Directory Project) is the most widespread one.

Graphics Digital pictures come in two flavors: raster graphics and vector graphics. Raster graphics or bitmaps are of a fixed size and simply encode the color of each pixel they contain. Usually, some kind of compression is supported. Lossy compression means that the image produced may differ slightly from the original, but it will generally require even less space than one encoded with lossless compression.

The most widespread raster image formats are GIF (Graphics Interchange Format), typically used for simple things like icons on the web, and JPEG (Joint Photographic Experts Group), featuring lossy compression particularly suited to photos. PNG (Portable Network Graphics) is intended to replace GIF. TIFF (Tag Image File Format) is commonly used in professional domains like publishing and medical imaging.

Vector graphics, by contrast, describe pictures through a series of instructions for drawing geometric shapes like lines and arcs. The advantage of this approach is that vector graphics can be magnified or printed at high resolution without any loss of quality. Standards like Postscript and PDF (Portable Document Format) support vector graphics and are frequently used for documents combining text, vector graphics, and raster graphics. SVG (Scalable Vector Graphics) is an XML-based format.

For audio, WAV (Wave file) has become a de facto standard even beyond the personal computers for which it was originally conceived. MP3 (MPEG-1 Audio Layer-3) employs lossy compression and has gained popularity primarily as a means for encoding music, but is now also used for spoken language.   **Audio**

Video formats are even more dependent on compression technology. The most important standards here are those developed by the Moving Picture Experts Group. MPEG-1 is commonly used for video files. DVDs (Digital Versatile Discs) employ MPEG-2. With the help of MPEG-4, audio and video objects can be composed into scenes, and relationships between those objects as well as possible user interactions can be specified. The purpose of SMIL (Synchronized Multimedia Integration Language), an XML-based standard for use on the web, also is to coordinate multimedia elements including video. H.323 is the prevalent standard for Internet-based video conferences.   **Video**

Descriptive information about physical or digital objects is called metadata. RDF (Resource Description Framework) is a standard based on XML for describing Internet resources. It specifies *how* to provide metadata.   **Metadata**

Dublin Core, by contrast, is a standard regarding *what* metadata to provide. It specifies a set of 15 metadata elements: title, creator, subject, description, publisher, contributor, date, type, format, identifier, source, language, relation, coverage, and rights. LOM (Learning Object Metadata), a metadata standard used for eLearning applications, supports specialized attributes like interaction style, grade level, and prerequisites.

Editing content on remote systems requires standards on how to access that content. Many document management systems support ODMA (Open Document Management Ap-   **Access**

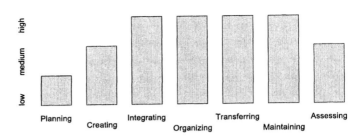

Figure 20.1. The contribution of standards to the various knowledge management processes.

plication Program Interface). WebDAV (World Wide Web Distributed Authoring and Versioning) is the leading standard for collaborative file management on the web.

Syndication   To syndicate content means to periodically supply material, usually on a subscription basis, to others who then reformat and integrate it with their own offerings. Newsfeeds are a typical example. RSS (RDF Site Summary) is a simple and popular standard for describing web content for syndication. NewsML, another standard based on XML, provides a more comprehensive set of features, including the distribution of multimedia and the ability to update content sent previously.

Relevance to Knowledge Management

Using standards and adhering to them is important for knowledge management mainly in two ways. First, it is of course a question of efficiency. This applies to internal efforts, and even more so when it comes to buying knowledge management tools from software vendors.

Second, being able to process content in standard formats allows organizations to tap the vast potential of knowledge being offered by content providers via the Internet. Like network technologies, standard formats therefore do not in themselves constitute direct applications of knowledge management, but they underpin many such applications in important ways.

Figure 20.1 shows the extent to which standards support the various knowledge management processes.

The planning phase is a highly individual effort for each organization and is usually conducted through face-to-face meetings. As such, it neither depends on standards nor do they have much to offer in support of it.

Planning

Knowledge creation does not stand to benefit very much from standards either. Perhaps some checklists may come in handy in order to ensure that important aspects are not forgotten, but on the whole ideal conditions for the creation of new knowledge call for as much freedom as possible, and not restrictions imposed through standards.

Creating

The one exception to this are technologies creating new content automatically based on existing content, such as expertise profiling. The use of standard formats for content naturally makes the task of such tools an easier one.

By contrast, standards are very important for integrating knowledge. The ability to automatically handle standardized exchange formats enables companies to efficiently integrate knowledge from outside sources, for example through content syndication.

Integrating

In managing the documented part of their own knowledge, companies will find it helpful to also adhere to standard formats internally from the beginning. This does not just apply to electronic documents, but equally to the metadata about those documents. Those metadata will ideally be assigned immediately during the integration process rather than later on. The range of metadata standards already developed and published by various organizations should prove useful for almost any business.

Organizing knowledge also stands to gain hugely from standards. Metadata may be assigned if it has not already been captured during integration, and has to be managed afterwards. Keeping documents in standard markup formats makes automated processing, for instance for the purposes of summarization and classification, much easier than performing those tasks with documents that are structured according to many different conventions.

Organizing

It is not only standards for the format of the content that have an impact on knowledge organization, however. Another kind of standards is equally important: Standard classification schemes from different sources ranging from national libraries and professional associations to online directories may either be directly adopted by companies for their internal purposes or they may serve as a basis which is then adapted to a company's specific needs.

Transferring

For knowledge transfer, standardized exchange formats are of course of major importance. This applies particularly to automated forms of knowledge transfer between different systems, but also to technology-mediated forms of communication between people. Metadata may not be quite as prominent here as in the two previous processes, but they do have a role to play in helping the receiver to recreate the original context of the knowledge being transferred.

Maintaining

Maintaining codified knowledge naturally will be a much easier task if all content is stored in a consistent manner based on explicitly specified standards. A suitable standard could, for instance, include an expiry date as a standard field in the metadata.

More generally, standards separating content from layout instructions will reduce the effort required for maintenance. Note that standards that already embody content in some form themselves, like classification schemes, have to be maintained as well. Since many of the published schemes are regularly being updated by their originating institutions, using those standards can take a lot of work off the shoulders of companies employing those schemes.

Assessing

To a certain extent, knowledge assessment may benefit from the use of standard formats for content because they can make it easier to automate at least a part of the assessment process. The values for most of the indicators used will typically still be assigned by hand, but when leveraging for instance expertise profiling technologies for knowledge assessment, the accuracy of the results may be better if the formats the content is stored in conforms to some standard known to the profiling software.

Issues

Thinking ahead

Technology is, as one of the lessons learned in chapter 3 emphasizes, a matter of pragmatism. Investing too much in efforts exceeding current requirements can be dangerous; software will often be replaced sooner rather than later anyway. When it comes to choosing appropriate file formats and adhering to standards, however, there is the danger of getting stuck in the long term by meeting specifications only barely. Here, just a little more effort may go a long way towards saving much in the future. After all, the issue here is how to store business-critical knowledge, for instance about customers, which will still be valuable when the software currently in use has long disappeared.

As a simple example, consider storing names in a database. There could be one field for the whole name of a person. If, however, at some point in the future one needs to access surnames, that will present a problem, since many people have more than one first name, and some also have surnames consisting of several parts separated by spaces, which makes surnames hard to extract automatically. With separate fields for first names and surnames this would not have happened.

The issue is thus not just to convert between different formats by mapping fields onto one another, but to go the extra mile of capturing distinctions which might prove useful in the future right from the start.

Looking at longer periods of time, particular attention has to be paid to the intelligibility of older formats to current software. The accessibility of a document in an archive will not be of much use if it cannot be displayed by available software. The fact that some software packages do not even understand the file formats of their own predecessors shows that this should not be taken lightly, especially when dealing with undocumented, proprietary formats.

Support of older formats

At the very least, electronic documents and appropriate software should therefore be archived together. The better solution, however, is to use standardized and well documented formats in the first place. Even if these should go out of fashion in the future, they will be much easier to convert.

Finally, one very general issue concerns the tradeoff between the benefits of standardizing and those of permitting users to choose for themselves. Declaring one format as the standard within the organization will bring many obvious benefits. The file format of a common word processing application, for instance, may be declared as the company-wide standard for all texts. Everybody will then always be able to read texts written by fellow employees.

Permitting choice

On the other hand, some people may have—or, in the course of time, develop—special requirements which are not being met by that particular software package, for example writers of technical documentation who need some more advanced features. There can, of course, be no general solution to this dilemma; the benefits of each approach have to be weighed against each other on a case-by-case basis. The issue does, however, again highlight the importance of taking a long-term view in choosing standards.

Chapter 21

Hardware

Just as information technology as a whole does not constitute the main focus of knowledge management, but rather acts as an enabler, hardware components are the prerequisite for any information technology support of knowledge management. This chapter first gives a brief overview of the kinds of hardware relevant to knowledge management, beginning with basic infrastructure and moving on to useful additions. After that, the relevance of hardware to the individual knowledge management processes is examined and some open issues are pointed out.

Overview

The most obvious components are of course the computers required to run any software. Servers and personal computers are complemented by mobile hardware such as notebook computers, personal digital assistants, and smartphones. The latter increasingly feature multimedia capabilities too.

Desktop and mobile devices

Hardware considerations regarding data storage are diverse. The issue here is not just speed of access, but also security. Equipment failures, natural disasters, and malicious acts such as theft need to be taken into account.

Storage

Storage therefore needs to be redundant. This will certainly include regular backups of critical data and may go as far as maintaining a fully operational data center at another geographical location, which can take over immediately in case of any trouble.

Providing a network infrastructure requires components

Network

ranging from switches to fiber optic cables to wireless base stations to communication satellites. Bandwidth, reliability, redundancy, and quality of service guarantees are central concerns here.

Input devices   Input devices are not limited to keyboards and mice. Special equipment is available for navigating the three-dimensional spaces employed by some advanced visualization techniques. Digital cameras are used to document what has been jotted down on flipcharts. Scanners make paper documents amenable to electronic processing. Microphones and digital video cameras provide alternative communication channels.

Output devices   Output devices include not just standard desktop screens, but range from small displays used for mobile applications to special purpose with particularly high resolution, for instance for viewing x-ray images. Video projectors are becoming more affordable all the time. New technologies are also emerging for three-dimensional displays. Finally, for audio output, speakers and headsets complement the range of available devices.

Combining input and output   Special-purpose hardware combining input and output facilities has been around for a long time in the form of phones and faxes. Today mobile phones are ubiquitous too, and there is also a market for videophones.

Some of the most interesting equipment combining input and output is not yet in widespread use, but is already shaping notions of what knowledge management could be like in the future. Smart walls are large wall-mounted displays interacting with groups of users. Augmented reality glasses are spectacles overlaying the real view with a computer-generated one and also function as an input device through eye-tracking.

Embedded systems   Generally, more and more computer hardware is embedded in items of daily use and in our surroundings. Wearable computing aims to embed all the mobile computing capacity one could need in clothing. Smart rooms not only feature smart walls, but also embedded systems which for instance permit the location of individuals in the room.

Relevance to Knowledge Management

The very first lessons learned in chapter 3 have been that knowledge management is primarily about people, and that it should be a holistic and comprehensive effort. An obvious consequence of this is that tools should support people in as

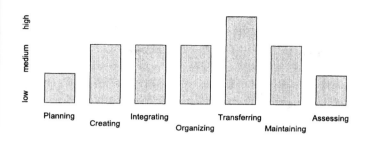

Figure 21.1. The contribution of hardware to the various knowledge management processes.

natural a way as possible, anytime, anywhere. The limiting factor here is, first of all, on the hardware side.

For example, people should not be required to return to their desks to complete a task just because that is where their personal computer is located. The natural thing would be for the tools to go where the people go. Thus mobile devices are playing an increasingly important role. One example particularly apt to show the relevance of such hardware for knowledge management are location based services: The focus here is on very context-specific knowledge, and such services obviously rely on mobile devices for delivering it.

Figure 21.1 shows the extent to which hardware supports the various knowledge management processes.

The planning phase is generally not very technology intensive, hence the role of special hardware for that process is correspondingly small.

Creating knowledge, by contrast, can benefit from particular hardware, even though technology does not play a central role here either. But hardware specifically suited for supporting group processes can have a positive impact. Smart walls are a very good example, but unfortunately also a very expensive one. On a more modest budget, a video projector connected to a computer may be very useful too. Beyond face-to-face settings, distributed teams engaging in knowledge creation may benefit from hardware such as cameras for video conferencing.

Knowledge integration can also benefit from specific hardware. For one thing, capturing knowledge in digital form today occurs mostly in the office. This is often simply due to the lack of mobile tools suited for that task in other locations.

Ideas, for instance, are best captured when and where they occur, which very often will not be in front of a desktop computer. A little waterproof gadget recording one's ideas under the shower may not be to everyone's liking, but mobile professionals like salespeople should be able to capture important knowledge on the spot, a point also emphasized by one of the lessons learned: Embed knowledge management in work processes rather than making them separate activities. This will result in a both quantitatively and qualitatively better knowledge repository: quantitatively, because some knowledge will be captured on the spot that would not have been input later at all, and qualitatively, because all knowledge being captured on the spot is less likely to lose details and context.

Desktop equipment does, however, have an impact as well. Since the paperless office has not arrived yet and does not seem likely to do so anytime soon, scanners are still needed to convert paper documents into electronic form.

The ability to organize knowledge well depends primarily on people and on software, not so much on hardware. However, since tasks like the automatic classification of documents tend to be computationally intensive, hardware considerations will play a role if high performance is an issue. Furthermore, advanced input and output devices make it easier to handle the large and complex structures typically involved in organizing knowledge.

Knowledge transfer often relies on the availability of specific hardware. Video conferencing obviously will not be possible without video cameras. Mobile devices usually have small displays, so their resolution becomes even more important. For some applications, one might indeed consider dispensing with the display altogether and using audio instead. While speech recognition is still far from perfect, especially in situations with high background noise, its quality has steadily improved over the years.

The overall importance of hardware for transferring knowledge is emphasized by one of the lessons learned: Offer multiple channels for knowledge transfer. This implies the availability of different input and output devices appropriate for the respective channels.

Hardware typically is not a major issue when it comes to maintaining knowledge. Only in the case of real-time knowledge maintenance do hardware considerations take on a more prominent role. This might be because content has to be updated by people on the road, which requires hardware for mobile access, or because complex operations have to be applied to huge quantities of content in a repository, which may raise performance issues and necessitate better servers.

Knowledge assessment, like knowledge planning, is generally not very technology-intensive. Consequently, hardware considerations will not play an important role here.

Assessing

Issues

Judging the appropriateness of particular hardware devices for knowledge management purposes directly addresses the lesson learned about the need to properly understand the knowledge requirements. What kind of knowledge is needed, when, and where? The user interface for most knowledge management software today is geared towards typical computer screens. However, smaller mobile devices like personal digital assistants and smartphones will increasingly be used for knowledge management tasks.

New kinds of hardware

The question arises which tasks can be sensibly performed on their small displays, which could be conducted through a speech interface, and which do not make sense at all on such devices. Network bandwidth, which has generally ceased to be an issue in office settings, is suddenly back with a vengeance as soon as wireless communication is being used.

On the other end of the spectrum, devices like video projectors are becoming more and more affordable and are therefore increasingly being used for knowledge management purposes in meetings. The user interfaces of most applications, however, are not ideal for a projected shared display. Summing up, new kinds of hardware are becoming available, but the best way to use them for knowledge management is often far from clear.

The lesson learned about the need to develop knowledge skills also applies to the new types of hardware. People are simply not used to have technologies supporting knowledge management everywhere, all the time. The spread of mobile phones has already raised many issues of how to use them appropriately, ranging from the hype around text messaging to issues of showing consideration for one's fellow human beings, for instance in restaurants.

New skills required

But all this is nothing yet compared to what can be expected for the future. With everyone connected everywhere and all the time, knowledge management will be possible in ways not dreamt of before, but at the same time conflicts of interest will arise where there were none before. Addressing these will require new skills on the part of the individual, and in the long run also new social norms.

Locator services   Finally, heeding the lesson learned to also take the built environment into consideration, the potential role of the kinds of hardware that make up intelligent buildings needs to be touched upon. Hardware for locating people within a building, for instance, can obviously aid knowledge management. However, the privacy issues related to this, as well as any other kind of technology that may be perceived as a surveillance mechanism, need to be addressed.

Chapter 22

Summary

Knowledge management is, first and foremost, a way of thinking. It is a way of thinking for managers: It draws attention to aspects which previously have often been neglected. In another sense, it is also a way of thinking for all employees: A knowledge-friendly culture increasingly determines the success of the company as a whole.

Like a pair of glasses, knowledge management brings some things into focus more sharply, things that one would otherwise have missed. On the other hand, glasses also restrict one's field of view: Knowledge management is no panacea for all problems that bedevil businesses today. These glasses simply complement the range already available and established in management.

In practical terms, knowledge management consists of a wealth of actions that can be taken to achieve business objectives. In order to better understand their possible uses and relationships, it helps to consider them through the lens of knowledge management processes.

Knowledge planning is concerned with knowledge management goals and strategies. Creating knowledge is all about generating new knowledge, while integrating knowledge refers to making both external and internal knowledge available to the entire company. Organizing knowledge superimposes a structure on available knowledge. Transferring knowledge includes both planned and unplanned communication of knowledge. Maintaining knowledge keeps knowledge available, accurate, and up to date. Assessing knowledge tackles the challenge of measuring knowledge.

The role of technology in knowledge management is that of an enabler. Knowledge management must not be driven by technology, but many technologies can make knowledge management both more effective and more efficient. Different technologies support each of the various knowledge management processes to a different extent (Figure 22.1).

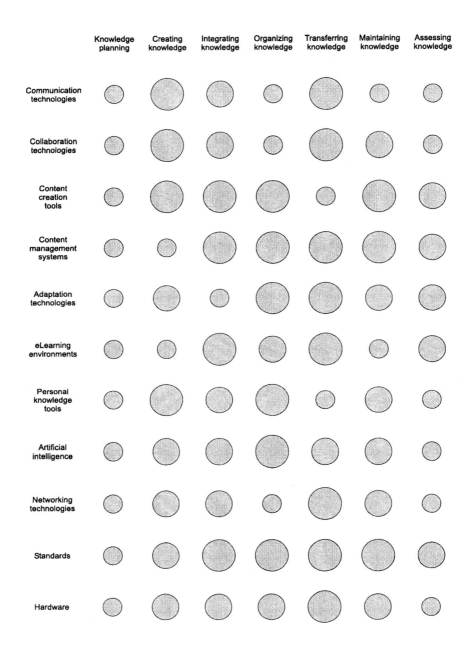

Figure 22.1.   The contribution of technologies to the various knowledge management processes.

Communication technologies such as email, electronic discussion forums, instant messaging, chatrooms, and video conferencing primarily support knowledge transfer. However, their contribution to knowledge creation should not be underestimated either: Creating knowledge heavily depends on communication, and participants may be geographically dispersed.

Collaboration technologies integrate communication technologies with further tools such as virtual whiteboards, brainstorming tools, voting mechanisms, and shared browsing. Again, knowledge transfer and knowledge creation benefit most from these technologies. Furthermore, workflow management systems support more structured forms of collaboration, which also benefits knowledge maintenance.

Content creation tools like authoring systems and annotation facilities help with creating and integrating knowledge, as do automated approaches to document enrichment and expertise profiling. Organizing knowledge benefits from specialized applications handling structures like thesauri and classifications schemes. All these tools not only help with creating content, but also with maintaining it.

Content management systems, including both document management and web content management, excel at integrating documented knowledge. Metadata and classification capabilities help with organizing knowledge, versioning and link management with maintaining it. Sophisticated retrieval functionality aids the transfer of knowledge.

Adaptation technologies like portals and recommender systems support the transfer of knowledge by making it possible to customize and personalize the presentation of content. In addition, visualization helps with managing the complex structures typically involved in organizing knowledge.

eLearning environments support knowledge transfer not only by helping learners to make sense of content, but also by enabling communication, both among learners and between learners and tutors. Testing components also make eLearning systems one of the few technologies that can directly help with assessing knowledge.

Personal knowledge tools support tasks ranging from note taking to bookmark management. These tools allow individuals to organize knowledge in accordance with their own mental models rather than structures established by others. For the same reason, personal knowledge tools also aid knowledge creation.

Artificial intelligence provides methods for automatically segmenting and classifying content, aiding the organization of knowledge. Expert systems and intelligent agents also support knowledge integration and knowledge transfer.

Network technologies rarely are at the foreground of any knowledge management initiative. Nevertheless, they provide necessary infrastructure and are particularly important with regard to knowledge transfer.

Standards for file exchange formats, metadata, and content syndication are important for knowledge integration, knowledge transfer, and knowledge maintenance. Organizing knowledge benefits from standards for specifying structures as well as from particular standardized structures such as library classification schemes.

Hardware, like network technologies, provides infrastructure required for other technologies. Suitable input and output devices, including video cameras and mobile devices, are particularly important for transferring knowledge.

Overall, transferring knowledge benefits most from technology, followed by integrating and organizing knowledge. Technology contributes very little to knowledge planning, and not a lot to assessing knowledge either.

Comparing the various technologies, content management supports a particularly broad range of knowledge management processes, as do content creation tools and standards. The latter two, in particular, merit more attention than is often being paid to them in practice.

This book has discussed knowledge management processes, supporting technologies, their relationships, and organizational and technological issues regarding their implementation as well as future research and development. Armed with this pair of glasses called knowledge management, you should now be able to see your organization in a new way, to spot improvement potentials, and to identify courses of action. Your own experiences with implementing those actions will constitute the fine finishing of your glasses.

Bibliography

[1] A. Abecker, A. Bernardi, K. Hinkelmann, O. Kühn, and M. Sintek. Toward a technology for organizational memories. *IEEE Intelligent Systems & Their Applications*, 13(3):40–48, May/June 1998.

[2] M. Alavi and D. E. Leidner. Knowledge management systems: Issues, challenges, and benefits. *Communications of the AIS*, 1(2), Feb. 1999.

[3] V. Allee. *The Knowledge Evolution: Expanding Organizational Intelligence.* Butterworth-Heinemann, Boston, 1997.

[4] V. Allee. The value evolution: Addressing larger implications of an intellectual capital and intangibles perspective. *Journal of Intellectual Capital*, 1(1):17–32, 2000.

[5] J. Ambrosio. Knowledge management mistakes. *Computerworld*, 34(27):44, 3 July 2000.

[6] D. M. Amidon. *Innovation Strategy for the Knowledge Economy: The Ken Awakening.* Butterworth-Heinemann, Boston, 1997.

[7] J. Angus. Behavior modification. *Knowledge Management Magazine*, July 1999.

[8] D. Apostolou and G. Mentzas. Managing corporate knowledge: A comparative analysis of experiences in consulting firms. In *PAKM 98. Proceedings of the Second International Conference on Practical Aspects of Knowledge Management*, pages 19/1–7, Zurich, Switzerland, 1998.

[9] W. Applehans, A. Globe, and G. Laugero. *Managing Knowledge: A Practical Web-Based Approach.* Addison-Wesley, Reading, MA, 1999.

[10] Using Information Technology to Support Knowledge Management. Consortium Benchmarking Study Final Report Executive Summary. American Productivity & Quality Center, 1997.

[11] A. Aurum, J. Cross, M. Handzic, and C. Van Toorn. Software support for creative problem solving. In T. Okamoto, R. Hartley, K. Klus, and J. P. Klus, editors, *Proceedings of the IEEE International Conference on Advanced Learning Technologies 2001*, pages 160–163, Aug. 2001.

[12] P. Balasubramanian, K. Nochur, J. C. Henderson, and M. M. Kwan. Managing process knowledge for decision support. *Decision Support Systems*, 27(1–2):145–162, Nov. 1999.

[13] C. M. Barlow. Insight or ideas: Escaping the idea centered "box" defining creativity. In *Proceedings of the 34th Annual Hawaii International Conference on Systems Sciences, HICSS-34*, pages 2877–2885, Los Alamitos, CA, USA, 2001. IEEE Computer Society.

[14] V. R. Benjamins, D. Fensel, and A. G. Pérez. Knowledge management through ontologies. In *PAKM 98. Proceedings of the Second International Conference on Practical Aspects of Knowledge Management*, pages 5/1–12, Zurich, Switzerland, 1998.

[15] M. A. Boden. Creativity and artificial intelligence. *Artificial Intelligence*, 103(1–2):347–356, Aug. 1998.

[16] E. Bolisani and E. Scarso. Information technology management: A knowledge-based perspective. *Technovation*, 19(4):209–217, Feb. 1999.

[17] N. Bontis. Assessing knowledge assets: A review of the models used to measure intellectual capital. *International Journal of Management Reviews*, 3(1):41–60, 2001.

[18] U. M. Borghoff and R. Pareschi. Information technology for knowledge management. *Journal of Universal Computer Science*, 3(8):835–842, 1997.

[19] R. P. Bostrom and M. Nagasundaram. Research in creativity and GSS. In *Proceedings of the 31st Annual Hawaii International Conference on Systems Sciences, HICSS-31*, volume 6, pages 391–405, Los Alamitos, CA, USA, 1998. IEEE Computer Society.

[20] A. Brooking. *Intellectual Capital: Core Asset for the Third Millennium*. International Thomson Business Press, London, 1996.

[21] A. Brooking. *Corporate Memory: Strategies for Knowledge Management*. International Thomson Business Press, London, 1999.

[22] I. Brown and L. Williams. Delivering 'information capability': The application of knowledge management in the defence library service. In *Information Online & On Disc 99: Strategies for the next millennium. Proceedings of the Ninth Australasian Information Online & On Disc Conference and Exhibition*, Sydney Convention and Exhibition Centre, Sydney, Australia, 19–21 Jan. 1999.

[23] J. S. Brown and P. Duguid. *The Social Life of Information*. Harvard Business School Press, Boston, Massachusetts, 2000.

[24] P. Browning and M. Lowndes. Content management systems. JISC Technology and Standards Watch Report TSW 01-02, Sept. 2001.

[25] J. Budzik and K. J. Hammond. Q&A: A system for the capture, organiation and reuse of expertise. In *Proceedings of the Sixty-second Annual Meeting of the American Society for Information Science*, Medford, NJ, 1999. Information Today, Inc.

[26] J. Budzik, K. J. Hammond, and L. Birnbaum. Information access in context. *Knowledge-Based Systems*, 14(1–2):37–53, Mar. 2001.

[27] W. R. Bukowitz and R. L. Williams. *Knowledge Management Fieldbook*. Financial Times/Prentice Hall, London, revised edition, 2000.

[28] P. R. Burden. *Knowledge Management: The Bibliography*. American Society for Information Science and Technology, 2000.

[29] M. Castells. *The Rise of the Network Society*, volume I of *The Information Age: Economy, Society and Culture*. Blackwell, Oxford, 2nd edition, 2000.

[30] T. Cerratto. Supporting collaborative writing and its cognitive tools. In K. Cox, B. Gorayska, and J. Marsh, editors, *Proceedings of the Third International Cognitive Technology Conference, CT'99*. Cognitive Technology Society, 1999.

[31] S. Chakrabarti, S. Srivastava, M. Subramanyam, and M. Tiwari. Using Memex to archive and mine community web browsing experience. *Computer Networks*, 33(1–6):669–684, June 2000.

[32] Z. Chen. Toward a better understanding of idea processors. *Information and Software Technology*, 40(10):541–553, Oct. 1998.

[33] C. W. Chong, T. Holden, P. Wilhelmij, and R. A. Schmidt. Where does knowledge management add value? *Journal of Intellectual Capital*, 1(4):366–380, 2000.

[34] D. Cohen and L. Prusak. British petroleum's virtual teamwork program. Case study, Ernst & Young Center for Business Innovation, June 1996.

[35] P. Cook. I heard it through the grapevine: Making knowledge management work by learning to share knowledge, skills and experience. *Industrial and Commercial Training*, 31(3):101–105, 1999.

[36] J. W. Cortada and J. A. Woods, editors. *The Knowledge Management Yearbook 1999–2000*. Butterworth-Heinemann, Boston, 1999.

[37] J. W. Cortada and J. A. Woods, editors. *The Knowledge Management Yearbook 2000–2001*. Butterworth-Heinemann, Boston, 2000.

[38] E. Crawford, J. Kay, and E. McCreath. An intelligent interface for sorting electronic mail. In *Proceedings of the 7th international conference on intelligent user interfaces*, pages 182–183. ACM Press, 2002.

[39] T. H. Davenport, D. W. de Long, and M. C. Beers. Successful knowledge management projects. *Sloan Management Review*, 39(2):43–57, Winter 1998.

[40] T. H. Davenport and L. Prusak. *Working Knowledge: How Organizations Manage What They Know*. Harvard Business School Press, Boston, MA, 1998.

[41] B. Davis and B. Riggs. Get smart. *Information Week*, 728:40–42, 46, 50, 5 Apr. 1999.

[42] G.-J. de Vreede, R. O. Briggs, R. van Duin, and B. Enserink. Athletics in electronic brainstorming: Asynchronous electronic brainstorming in very large groups. In R. H. Sprague, Jr., editor, *Proceedings of the 33rd Annual Hawaii International Conference on Systems Sciences, HICSS-33*, pages 331–341, Los Alamitos, CA, USA, 2000. IEEE Computer Society.

[43] S. Denning. Seven basics of knowledge management. *Communication Technology Decisions*, Autumn/Winter 1999.

[44] C. Despres and D. Chauvel. Knowledge management(s). *Journal of Knowledge Management*, 3(2):110–120, 1999.

[45] C. Despres and D. Chauvel, editors. *Knowledge Horizons: The Present and the Promise of Knowledge Management*. Butterworth-Heinemann, Boston, 2000.

[46] G. Disterer. Individual and social barriers to knowledge transfer. In *Proceedings of the 34th Annual Hawaii International Conference on Systems Sciences, HICSS-34*, pages 3008–3014, Los Alamitos, CA, USA, 2001. IEEE Computer Society.

[47] N. M. Dixon. *Common Knowledge: How Companies Thrive by Sharing What They Know*. Harvard Business School Press, Boston, MA, 2000.

[48] P. Dourish, J. Lamping, and T. Rodden. Building bridges: Customisation and mutual intelligibility in shared category management. In *Proceedings of the International Conference on Supporting Group Work, GROUP'99*, pages 11–20. ACM Press, 1999.

[49] S. Drew. Building knowledge management into strategy: Making sense of a new perspective. *Long Range Planning*, 32(1):130–136, Feb. 1999.

[50] G. Droschl. Was leisten Informationssysteme im Wissensmanagement? In M. Bornemann and M. Sammer, editors, *Anwendungsorientiertes Wissensmanagement: Ansätze und Fallstudien aus der betrieblichen und der universitären Praxis*, Gabler Edition Wissenschaft, chapter 13, pages 225–245. Deutscher Universitäts-Verlag, Wiesbaden, 2002.

[51] P. F. Drucker. Knowledge-worker productivity: The biggest challenge. *California Management Review*, 41(2):79–94, 1999.

[52] L. Edvinsson and M. S. Malone. *Intellectual Capital: Realizing Your Company's True Value by Finding Its Hidden Brainpower*. Harper Business, New York, 1997.

[53] L. Fahey and L. Prusak. The eleven deadliest sins of knowledge management. *California Management Review*, 40(3):265–276, Spring 1998.

[54] W. Fan, M. D. Gordon, and P. Pathak. Personalization of search engine services for effective retrieval and knowledge management. In *Proceedings of the 21st Annual International Conference on Information Systems (ICIS2000)*, pages 20–34, 2000.

[55] S. Feldman. Meaning-based search tools: Find what I mean, not what I say. *Online*, 24(3), May 2000.

[56] M. H. Friedman. Barrier bashing. *Intelligent Enterprise*, 3(10):68–72, 2000.

[57] P. Gentsch. *Wissen managen mit moderner Informationstechnologie: Strategien, Werkzeuge, Praxisbeispiele*. Gabler, Wiesbaden, 1999.

[58] A. J. Godbout. Filtering Knowledge: Changing Information into Knowledge Assets. Technical Report 9867, Godbout Martin Godbout & ass., 1998.

[59] A. J. Godbout. State of the KM art: Lessons learned from Early Adoptions of Knowledge Management. Technical Report 99103, Godbout Martin Godbout & ass., 1999.

[60] M. Goebel and L. Gruenwald. A survey of data mining and knowledge discovery software tools. *SIGKDD Explorations*, 1(1):20–33, June 1999.

[61] P. C. Green. *Building Robust Competencies: Linking Human Resource Systems to Organizational Strategies.* Jossey-Bass, San Francisco, 1999.

[62] O. Gupta and G. Roos. Mergers and acquisitions through an intellectual capital perspective. *Journal of Intellectual Capital,* 2(3):297–309, 2001.

[63] D. Gurteen. Knowledge, creativity and innovation. *Journal of Knowledge Management,* 2(1):5–13, Sept. 1998.

[64] J. Hahn and M. R. Subramani. A framework of knowledge management systems: Issues and challenges for theory and practice. In *Proceedings of the 21st Annual International Conference on Information Systems (ICIS2000),* pages 302–312, 2000.

[65] W. E. Halal, editor. *The Infinite Resource: Creating and Leading the Knowledge Enterprise.* Jossey-Bass, San Francisco, 1998.

[66] M. T. Hansen, N. Nohria, and T. Tierney. What's your strategy for managing knowledge? *Harvard Business Review,* 77(2):106–116, Mar./Apr. 1999.

[67] *Harvard Business Review on Knowledge Management.* Harvard Business School Press, Boston, MA, 1998.

[68] M. Hauer. Three thousand years of knowledge management: What can we learn from science? *Information Services & Use,* 19(1):37–44, 1999.

[69] S. Hauschild, T. Licht, and W. Stein. Creating a knowledge culture. *McKinsey Quarterly,* 1:74–81, 2001.

[70] U. Heckert. *Informations- und Kommunikationstechnologie beim Wissensmanagement: Gestaltungsmodell für die industrielle Produktentwicklung.* Deutscher Universitäts-Verlag, Wiesbaden, 2002.

[71] T. Hedesstrom and E. A. Whitley. What is meant by tacit knowledge? Towards a better understanding of the shape of actions. In H. R. Hansen, M. Bichler, and H. Mahrer, editors, *ECIS 2000: A Cyberspace Odyssey. Proceedings of the 8th European Conference on Information Systems,* volume 1, pages 46–51, Vienna, Austria, July 2000. Vienna University of Economics and Business Administration.

[72] E. Heinrich and H. Maurer. Active documents: Concept, implementation and applications. *Journal of Universal Computer Science,* 6(12):1197–1202, 2000.

[73] J. M. Hender, T. L. Rodgers, D. L. Dean, and J. F. Nunamaker, Jr. Improving group creativity: Brainstorming versus non-brainstorming techniques in a GSS environment. In *Proceedings of the 34th Annual Hawaii International Conference on Systems Sciences, HICSS-34,* pages 527–536, Los Alamitos, CA, USA, 2001. IEEE Computer Society.

[74] D. Hicks and K. Tochtermann. Personal digital libraries and knowledge management. *Journal of Universal Computer Science,* 7(7):550–565, 2001.

[75] C. Hildebrand. Making KM pay off. *CIO Enterprise Magazine,* pages 64–66, 15 Feb. 1999.

[76] G. Hodge. Systems of knowledge organization for digital libraries: Beyond traditional authority files. Technical Report pub91, The Digital Library Federation Council on Library and Information Resources, Washington DC, Apr. 2000.

[77] C. W. Holsapple and K. D. Joshi. An investigation of factors that influence the management of knowledge in organizations. *The Journal of Strategic Information Systems*, 9(2–3):235–261, Sept. 2000.

[78] H. Hsieh and F. M. Shipman III. VITE: A visual interface supporting the direct manipulation of structured data using two-way mappings. In *Proceedings of the 2000 International Conference on Intelligent User Interfaces*, pages 141–148, 2000.

[79] M. Huysman, D. de Wit, and E. Andriessen. A critical evaluation of the practice of knowledge management. Paper presented at the ECSCW'99 Workshop "Beyond Knowledge Management: Managing Expertise". 6th European Conference on Computer Supported Cooperative Work, 1999.

[80] J. Ismail. The design of an e-learning system: Beyond the hype. *The Internet and Higher Education*, 4(3–4):329–336, 2001.

[81] B. J. Jansen and U. Pooch. A review of web searching studies and a framework for future research. *Journal of the American Society of Information Science and Technology*, 52(3):235–246, Feb. 2001.

[82] B. Junnarkar. Leveraging collective intellect by building organizational capabilities. *Expert Systems with Applications*, 13(1):29–39, July 1997.

[83] B. Junnarkar and C. V. Brown. Re-assessing the enabling role of information technology in KM. *Journal of Knowledge Management*, 1(2):142–148, Dec. 1997.

[84] J. M. Kamara, C. J. Anumbab, and P. M. Carrillo. A CLEVER approach to selecting a knowledge management strategy. *International Journal of Project Management*, 20(3):205–211, Apr. 2002.

[85] R. S. Kaplan and D. P. Norton. Using the balanced scorecard as a strategic management system. *Harvard Business Review*, pages 75–85, Jan./Feb. 1996.

[86] S. Kelly and M. Jones. Groupware and the social infrastructure of communication. *Communications of the ACM*, 44(12):77–79, Dec. 2001.

[87] L. L. Kemp, K. E. Nidiffer, L. C. Rose, R. Small, and M. Stankosky. Knowledge management: Insights from the trenches. *IEEE Software*, 18(6):66–68, Nov./Dec. 2001.

[88] B. Kitts, L. Edvinsson, and T. Beding. Intellectual capital: From intangible assets to fitness landscapes. *Expert Systems with Applications*, 20(1):35–50, Jan. 2001.

[89] D. A. Klein, editor. *The Strategic Management of Intellectual Capital*. Butterworth-Heinemann, Oxford, 1998.

[90] A.-T. Koh. Linking learning, knowledge creation, and business creativity: A preliminary assessment of the East Asian quest for creativity. *Technological Forecasting and Social Change*, 64(1):85–100, May 2000.

[91] T. M. Koulopoulos and C. Frappaolo. *Smart Things to Know About Knowledge Management*. Capstone Press, Dover, NH, 1999.

[92] R. Kremer. Visual languages for knowledge representation. In *Proceedings of KAW'98: Eleventh Workshop on Knowledge Acquisition, Modeling and Management*, Voyager Inn, Banff, Alberta, Canada, 18–23 Apr. 1998.

[93] U. Krohn, N. J. Davies, and R. Weeks. Concept lattices for knowledge management. *BT Technology Journal*, 17(4):108–116, Oct. 1999.

[94] O. Kühn and A. Abecker. Corporate memories for knowledge management in industrial practice: Prospects and challenges. *Journal of Universal Computer Science*, 3(8):929–954, 1997.

[95] R. C. W. Kwok and M. Khalifa. Effect of GSS on knowledge acquisition. *Information & Management*, 34(6):307–315, 21 Dec. 1998.

[96] K. La Barre and C. Dent. Creating conceptual access: Faceted knowledge organization in the unrev-ii email archives. In *Proceedings of the 10th International Conference on Conceptual Structures (ICCS 2002): Integration and Interfaces*, 2002.

[97] H. Lai and T. H. Chu. Knowledge management: A review of theoretical frameworks and industrial cases. In R. H. Sprague, Jr., editor, *Proceedings of the 33rd Annual Hawaii International Conference on Systems Sciences, HICSS-33*, pages 925–934, Los Alamitos, CA, USA, 2000. IEEE Computer Society.

[98] J. R. Landry. Forgetful or bad memory? In *Proceedings of the 32nd Annual Hawaii International Conference on Systems Sciences, HICSS-32*, Los Alamitos, CA, USA, 1999. IEEE Computer Society.

[99] J. R. Landry. Playing at learning: Why knowledge creation needs fun. In R. H. Sprague, Jr., editor, *Proceedings of the 33rd Annual Hawaii International Conference on Systems Sciences, HICSS-33*, pages 983–989, Los Alamitos, CA, USA, 2000. IEEE Computer Society.

[100] F. Lehner. *Organisational Memory: Konzepte und Systeme für das organisatorische Lernen und das Wissensmanagement.* Hanser, München, 2000.

[101] K.-H. Leitner, K. Grasenick, H. Haubold, T. Jud, F. Ohler, F. Pirker, and H. Rollett. Development of a knowledge accounting system. Technical report, Forschung Austria, Vienna, Austria, 2000.

[102] D. Leonard. *Wellsprings of Knowledge: Building and Sustaining the Sources of Innovation.* Harvard Business School Press, Boston, MA, 1998.

[103] J. H. Leuthold. Is computer-based learning right for everyone? In *Proceedings of the 32nd Annual Hawaii International Conference on Systems Sciences, HICSS-32*, Los Alamitos, CA, USA, 1999. IEEE Computer Society.

[104] T. Ley, H. Rollett, G. Dösinger, K. Tochtermann, K. Bruhnsen, and G. Droschl. Implementing instruments for managing intellectual capital: 3 case studies and some lessons learned. In *Proceedings of the Third European Conference on Knowledge Management*, pages 400–412, Nr Reading, England, Sept. 2002. Management Centre International Limited.

[105] X. Lin and L. M. Chan. Personalized knowledge organization and access for the web. *Library & Information Science Research*, 21(2):153–172, 1999.

[106] A. Lococo and D. C. Yen. Groupware: Computer supported collaboration. *Telematics and Informatics*, 15(1–2):85–101, Feb. 1998.

[107] K.-M. Lugger and H. Kraus. Mastering the human barriers in knowledge management. *Journal of Universal Computer Science*, 7(6):488–497, 2001.

[108] M. L. Mackenzie. The personal organization of electronic mail messages in a business environment: An exploratory study. *Library & Information Science Research*, 22(4):405–426, Nov. 2000.

[109] R. Maier and U. Remus. Towards a framework for knowledge management strategies: Process orientation as strategic starting point. In *Proceedings of the 34th Annual Hawaii International Conference on Systems Sciences, HICSS-34*, pages 1459–1468, Los Alamitos, CA, USA, 2001. IEEE Computer Society.

[110] A. D. Marwick. Knowledge management technology. *IBM Systems Journal*, 40(4):814–830, 2001.

[111] S. Masterton and S. Watt. Oracles, bards, and village gossips, or social roles and meta knowledge management. *Information Systems Frontiers*, 2(3/4):299–315, 2000.

[112] H. Maurer. Web-based knowledge management. *Computer*, 31(3):122–123, Mar. 1998.

[113] H. Maurer and K. Tochtermann. On a new powerful model for knowledge management and its applications. *Journal of Universal Computer Science*, 8(1):85–96, 2002.

[114] R. McAdam and S. McCreedy. A critical review of knowledge management models. *The Learning Organization*, 6(3):91–101, 1999.

[115] R. McDermott. Why information technology inspired but cannot deliver knowledge management. *California Management Review*, 41(4):103–117, Summer 1999.

[116] E. McFadzean. Techniques to enhance creative thinking. *Team Performance Management*, 6(3/4):62–72, 2000.

[117] P. Meso and R. Smith. A resource-based view of organizational knowledge management systems. *Journal of Knowledge Management*, 4(3):224–234, 2000.

[118] J. Mullich. Growing a knowledge management solution. *Knowledge Management Magazine*, Mar. 2001.

[119] I. Nonaka and H. Takeuchi. *The Knowledge-Creating Company: How Japanese Companies Create the Dynamics of Innovation*. Oxford University Press, New York, Oxford, 1995.

[120] I. Nonaka, R. Toyama, and N. Konno. SECI, ba and leadership: A unified model of dynamic knowledge creation. *Long Range Planning*, 33(1):5–34, Feb. 2000.

[121] K. North. *Wissensorientierte Unternehmensführung: Wertschöpfung durch Wissen*. Gabler, Wiesbaden, 2nd edition, 1999.

[122] K. North and N. Varlese. Motivieren für die Wissensteilung und die Wissensentwicklung. *Wissensmanagement*, Jan. 2001.

[123] C. S. O'Dell and C. J. Grayson. Identifying and Transferring Internal Best Practices. White Paper, American Productivity & Quality Center, 1997.

[124] C. S. O'Dell, C. J. Grayson, Jr., and N. Essaides. *If Only We Knew What We Know: The Transfer of Internal Knowledge and Best Practice.* The Free Press, New York, 1998.

[125] H. Ohiwa, N. Takeda, K. Kawai, and A. Shiomi. KJ Editor: A card-handling tool for creative work support. *Knowledge-Based Systems*, 10(1):43–50, June 1997.

[126] M. Parent, R. B. Gallupe, W. D. Salisbury, and J. M. Handelmand. Knowledge creation in focus groups: Can group technologies help? *Information & Management*, 38(1):47–58, Oct. 2000.

[127] C. Prichard, R. Hull, M. Chumer, and H. Willmott, editors. *Managing Knowledge: Critical Investigations of Work and Learning.* Macmillan Business, London, 2000.

[128] G. Probst, S. Raub, and K. Romhardt. *Wissen managen: Wie Unternehmen ihre wertvollste Ressource optimal nutzen.* FAZ Verlag/Gabler, Frankfurt am Main, Wiesbaden, third edition, 1999.

[129] G. J. B. Probst. Practical knowledge management: A model that works. *Arthur D. Little Prism*, pages 17–29, Second Quarter 1998.

[130] L. Prusak, editor. *Knowledge in Organizations.* Resources for the Knowledge-Based Economy. Butterworth-Heinemann, Boston, 1997.

[131] D. Ramhorst. A guided tour through the Siemens Business Services knowledge management framework. *Journal of Universal Computer Science*, 7(7):610–622, 2001.

[132] V. M. Ribière. The role of organizational culture in KM initiatives' successes. In D. Remenyi, editor, *Proceedings of the Second European Conference on Knowledge Management*, pages 523–539, Nr Reading, England, Nov. 2001. Management Centre International Limited.

[133] M. Robertson, C. Sørensen, and J. Swan. Facilitating knowledge creation with groupware: A case study of a knowledge intensive firm. In R. H. Sprague, Jr., editor, *Proceedings of the 33rd Annual Hawaii International Conference on Systems Sciences, HICSS-33*, pages 240–248, Los Alamitos, CA, USA, 2000. IEEE Computer Society.

[134] H. Rollett. Implikationen von Praxiserfahrungen für die IT-Unterstützung von Wissensmanagement. In M. Bornemann and M. Sammer, editors, *Anwendungsorientiertes Wissensmanagement: Ansätze und Fallstudien aus der betrieblichen und der universitären Praxis*, Gabler Edition Wissenschaft, chapter 15, pages 275–294. Deutscher Universitäts-Verlag, Wiesbaden, 2002.

[135] H. Rollett, T. Ley, and K. Tochtermann. Supporting knowledge creation: Towards a tool for explicating and sharing mental models. In D. Remenyi, editor, *Proceedings of the Second European Conference on Knowledge Management*, pages 569–582, Nr Reading, England, Nov. 2001. Management Centre International Limited.

[136] J. Roos, G. Roos, N. C. Dragonetti, and L. Edvinsson. *Intellectual Capital: Navigating the New Business Landscape.* Macmillan Business, London, 1997.

[137] J. Rowley. Knowledge organisation for a new millennium: Principles and processes. *Journal of Knowledge Management*, 4(3):217–223, 2000.

[138] J. Rowley. Knowledge organisation in a web-based environment. *Management Decision*, 39(5):355–361, 2001.

[139] R. L. Ruggles, editor. *Knowledge Management Tools*. Resources for the Knowledge-Based Economy. Butterworth-Heinemann, Boston, 1997.

[140] C. M. Savage. *Fifth Generation Management: Co-Creating Through Virtual Enterprising, Dynamic Teaming, and Knowledge Networking*. Butterworth-Heinemann, Boston, 1996.

[141] R. C. Schank. Revolutionizing the traditional classroom course. *Communications of the ACM*, 44(12):21–24, Dec. 2001.

[142] D. G. Schwartz. When email meets organizational memories: Addressing threats to communication in a learning organization. *International Journal of Human Computer Studies*, 51(3):599–614, Sept. 1999.

[143] P. Seemann. Real-world knowledge management: What's working for Hoffman-LaRoche. Case study, Ernst & Young Center for Business Innovation, 1996.

[144] P. M. Senge. *The Fifth Discipline Fieldbook: Strategies and Tools for Building a Learning Organization*. Doubleday, New York, 1994.

[145] P. M. Senge. *The Fifth Discipline: The Art and Practice of the Learning Organization*. Doubleday, New York, 1994.

[146] M. Shin, T. Holden, and R. A. Schmidt. From knowledge theory to management practice: Towards an integrated approach. *Information Processing & Management*, 37(2):335–355, 2001.

[147] B. Shneiderman. Supporting creativity with advanced information-abundant user interfaces. Position Paper for National Science Foundation and European Commission meeting on human-computer interaction research agenda, 1–4 June 1999, Toulouse, France, 1999.

[148] A. Sigel. Towards knowledge organization with topic maps. In *Proceedings of XML Europe 2000*, pages 603–611, Alexandria, VA, 2000. Graphic Communications Association.

[149] A. J. Slade and A. F. Bokma. Conceptual approaches for personal and corporate information and knowledge management. In *Proceedings of the 34th Annual Hawaii International Conference on Systems Sciences, HICSS-34*, pages 418–425, Los Alamitos, CA, USA, 2001. IEEE Computer Society.

[150] M. Smith, J. J. Cadiz, and B. Burkhalter. Conversation trees and threaded chats. In *Proceedings of the 2000 ACM Conference on Computer Supported Cooperative Work*, pages 97–105, 2000.

[151] R. G. Smith and A. Farquhar. The road ahead for knowledge management. *AI Magazine*, 21(4):17–40, Winter 2000.

[152] T. K. Srikantaiah and M. E. D. Koenig, editors. *Knowledge Management for the Information Professional*. ASIS Monograph Series. Information Today, Medford, New Jersey, 2000.

[153] D. Stenmark. Company-wide brainstorming: Next generation suggestion systems? In L. Svensson, U. Snis, C. Sørensen, H. Fägerlind, T. Lindrotha, M. Magnusson, and C. Östlund, editors, *Proceedings of IRIS 23*. Laboratorium for Interaction Technology, University of Trollhättan Uddevalla, 2000.

[154] D. Stenmark. The creative intranet: Factors for corporate knowledge creation. In L. Svensson, U. Snis, C. Sørensen, H. Fägerlind, T. Lindrotha, M. Magnusson, and C. Östlund, editors, *Proceedings of IRIS 23*. Laboratorium for Interaction Technology, University of Trollhättan Uddevalla, 2000.

[155] T. A. Stewart. *Intellectual Capital: The New Wealth of Organizations*. Currency Doubleday, New York, 1997.

[156] J. Storey and E. Barnett. Knowledge management initiatives: Learning from failure. *Journal of Knowledge Management*, 4(2):145–156, 2000.

[157] K. E. Sveiby. *The New Organizational Wealth: Managing and Measuring Knowledge-Based Assets*. Berrett-Koehler, San Francisco, 1997.

[158] J. Swan, S. Newell, and M. Robertson. Limits of IT-driven knowledge management initiatives for interactive innovation processes: Towards a community-based approach. In R. H. Sprague, Jr., editor, *Proceedings of the 33rd Annual Hawaii International Conference on Systems Sciences, HICSS-33*, pages 84–94, Los Alamitos, CA, USA, 2000. IEEE Computer Society.

[159] R. J. Thierauf. *Knowledge Management Systems for Business*. Quorum, Westport, Connecticut, 1999.

[160] J. Thomas, P. Cowley, O. Kuchar, L. Nowell, J. Thomson, and P. C. Wong. Discovering knowledge through visual analysis. *Journal of Universal Computer Science*, 7(6):517–529, 2001.

[161] A. Tiwana. *The Knowledge Management Toolkit: Practical Techniques for Building a Knowledge Management System*. Prentice Hall PTR, Upper Saddle River, NJ, 2000.

[162] K. Tochtermann, T. Ley, and H. Rollett. Wissensmanagement, Management intellektuellen Kapitals und eLearning: Alleinstellungsmerkmale und Zusammenhänge. In K. Bauknecht, W. Brauer, and T. Mück, editors, *Informatik 2001, Tagungsband der GI/OCG-Jahrestagung*, volume 1, pages 34–40, Wien, Sept. 2001. Österreichische Computer Gesellschaft.

[163] E. Tsui. Exploring the KM toolbox. *Knowledge Management*, 4(2):11–14, Oct. 2000.

[164] I. Tuomi. Data is more than knowledge: Implications of the reversed knowledge hierarchy for knowledge management and organizational memory. In *Proceedings of the 32nd Annual Hawaii International Conference on Systems Sciences, HICSS-32*, Los Alamitos, CA, USA, 1999. IEEE Computer Society.

[165] R. P. uit Beijerse. Knowledge management in small and medium-sized companies: Knowledge management for entrepreneurs. *Journal of Knowledge Management*, 4(2):162–179, 2000.

[166] A. Vincent and D. Ross. Personalize training: Determine learning styles, personality types and multiple intelligences online. *The Learning Organization*, 8(1):36–43, 2001.

[167] H. F. O. von Kortzfleisch and U. Winand. Trust in electronic learning and teaching relationships: The case of "WINFO-Line". In H. R. Hansen, M. Bichler, and H. Mahrer, editors, *ECIS 2000: A Cyberspace Odyssey. Proceedings of the 8th European Conference on Information Systems*, volume 2, pages 1348–1354, Vienna, Austria, July 2000. Vienna University of Economics and Business Administration.

[168] G. von Krogh, K. Ichijo, and I. Nonaka. *Enabling Knowledge Creation: How to Unlock the Mystery of Tacit Knowledge and Release the Power of Innovation.* Oxford University Press, New York, 2000.

[169] G. von Krogh, I. Nonaka, and M. Aben. Making the most of your company's knowledge: A strategic framework. *Long Range Planning*, 34(4):421–439, Aug. 2001.

[170] L. von Rosenstiel, W. Molt, and B. Rüttinger. *Organisationspsychologie*, volume 22 of *Grundriß der Psychologie*. W. Kohlhammer, Stuttgart, 8th edition, 1995.

[171] H. D. Wactlar. Extracting and visualizing knowledge from film and video archives. *Journal of Universal Computer Science*, 8(6):602–612, 2002.

[172] G. Walsham. Knowledge management: The benefits and limitations of computer systems. *European Management Journal*, 19(6):599–608, Dec. 2001.

[173] C.-P. Wei and Y.-X. Dong. A mining-based category evolution approach to managing online document categories. In *Proceedings of the 34th Annual Hawaii International Conference on Systems Sciences, HICSS-34*, pages 2669–2678, Los Alamitos, CA, USA, 2001. IEEE Computer Society.

[174] E. Wenger. Communities of practice: Learning as a social system. *Systems Thinker*, 9(5), June/July 1998.

[175] K. M. Wiig. What future knowledge management users may expect. *Journal of Knowledge Management*, 3(2):155–165, 1999.

[176] D. Wolfram, A. Spink, B. J. Jansen, and T. Saracevic. Vox populi: The public searching of the web. *Journal of the American Society of Information Science and Technology*, 52(12):1073–1074, Dec. 2001.

[177] Workflow Management Coalition. Terminology & Glossary (Issue 3.0). Technical Report WFMC-TC-1011, Workflow Management Coalition, Winchester, UK, Feb. 1999.

[178] M. H. Zack. Developing a knowledge strategy. *California Management Review*, 41(3):125–145, Spring 1999.

[179] M. H. Zack. Managing codified knowledge. *Sloan Management Review*, 40(4):45–58, Summer 1999.

[180] H. Zantout and F. Marir. Document management systems from current capabilities towards intelligent information retrieval: An overview. *International Journal of Information Management*, 19(6):471–484, Dec. 1999.

Index

225

About the Author

Herwig Rollett conducts research and industry projects at the Know-Center, Austria's competence center for knowledge based applications and systems. He is also vice chairman of the Wissensmanagement Forum, a nonprofit association dedicated to knowledge management. Previously, he has been engaged in knowledge management research at the Institute for Information Processing and Computer Supported New Media, Graz University of Technology; and Forschung Austria, the umbrella organization of the country's largest non-university research institutions. He can be contacted at `wig@acm.org`.